WHO'S BU

Who's Bugging You?

Inside Ireland's Secret World of Electronic Surveillance

BRENDAN MUNNELLY

THE MERCIER PRESS
CORK and DUBLIN

The Mercier Press Limited
4 Bridge Street, Cork
24 Lower Abbey Street, Dublin 1

British Library Cataloguing in Publication Data
Munnelly, Brendan
  Who's bugging you?
  1. Eavesdropping – Ireland 2. Electronic intelligence
  3. Espionage – Ireland 4. Electronic intelligence
  I. Title
  384   HV6295.173

ISBN 0-85342-784-4

To all my families

Printed by Litho Press Co., Midleton, Co. Cork.

Contents

PART I : A Tap on the Line

PART II : A Bug in the Room

PART III : A Spy in the Sky

Acknowledgements

This book may be compared to a patchwork quilt for which many others have supplied both the individual pieces and the connecting threads which draw them together into a coherent whole. Given its subject matter the mentioning of names might be regarded as an invidious distinction. I am grateful nonetheless.

Two names which can be recorded are those of journalists Duncan Campbell and Frank Doherty. It was Campbell's exposé in 1977 of Britain's electronic espionage activities that first exercised my interest in such matters and his continuing work at the *New Statesman* magazine never disappoints.

Nearer home, Frank Doherty has over the years blazed an investigative trail into many of the subjects covered in this book. For his generous assistance and general guidance, I express my indebtedness.

Many others supplied invaluable help with materials and sources, ideas and comments, time and effort, hardware and software. Again, much thanks.

I must also thank in advance anyone who kindly points out any errors of fact or logic in this book. My intention is to stimulate debate and interest in the topics covered herein — and not to claim the final word.

And last but not least to Geraldine, without whose enthusiasm this book could not have begun and without whose forbearance it would never have been finished. Thanks.

Foreword

On 12 January 1987, two Dublin-based journalists walked out of the High Court, £40,000 richer than when they entered. Almost three years after they launched their Constitutional action, Bruce Arnold and Geraldine Kennedy had been successful in claiming that their rights to privacy had been infringed by a previous Fianna Fáil government, under which their telephones had been tapped. The High Court directed that the tapes of their intercepted conversations be returned to them and that they each be awarded £20,000 in damages for the distress so inflicted.

In a reserved judgement, Mr Justice Hamilton said: 'The action of the Executive in this case in tapping the telephones of the plaintiffs without any lawful justification and in interfering with and intruding upon the privacy of the plaintiffs constituted an attack on their dignity and freedom as individuals and journalists and cannot be tolerated in a democratic society such as ours is and our Constitution requires it to be.'

In September 1982 it was revealed by the *Irish Times* that two journalists, Kennedy and Arnold, had had their telephones tapped on the orders of a Fianna Fáil Minister for Justice, Seán Doherty. The former minister, as he then was, said that cabinet leaks justified this action.

This controversy was still simmering when another surveillance scandal shocked the public. A family with no connection with public life except a personal friendship with SDLP politician Seamus Mallon, the Moynas, found that their house had been bugged with a listening device.

Both cases raise the question of the invasion of the privacy of private citizens by the state without the knowledge or consent of those citizens. If the telephones of journalists can be tapped, if listening devices can be left in people's houses by persons purporting to work for Telecom Éireann, whose privacy is safe? What protection has the private citizen against this kind of invasion of his or her privacy? How far does recent legislation go in providing such protection?

Less headline-catching, but even more sinister were a number of revelations that meetings of workers were being eavesdropped on by their employers without the former's knowledge or consent.

Few people understand what new technology has made possible in terms of surveillance. Even fewer realise how readily it is available, not only to state agencies, but to a range of 'private investigators' and agents involved in industrial espionage and domestic investigations.

What can the individual do to protect his or her privacy against electronic invasion? Is there legislation to protect it? Will the state take measures to afford this protection if it restricts its own powers? These are some of the questions considered in this book.

Part One of this book deals with telephone-tapping: how it began; who does it; how and where they do it; and – an important if much neglected point – whether it is legal. The history of telephone-tapping in this country is one which is long, controversial and punctuated with scandal. It is also a largely secret history. Its protagonists, from the Dublin Metropolitan Police of the late nineteenth century to the army and garda officers of today, could never be accused of publicity seeking. But where there is not public knowledge, there is no guarantee of public control.

The increasing use by private detective and investigation agencies of bugging and other electronic eavesdropping devices is another area which has given rise to some disquiet. As well it might – given the number of extraordinary episodes of recent years, variously set in factory canteens and offices, boardrooms and bedrooms. Part Two of this book chronicles this mushrooming growth of electronic snooping in Ireland.

Yet to present the Irish state and its various security agencies as invaders of privacy is to present only half the picture. As Part Three of this book details, the state is itself also a victim of electronic surveillance. Listening in are the eavesdroppers of Britain's Government Communications Headquarters (GCHQ) and the National Security Agency (NSA) of the United States, which actively monitor telephone and other communications passing in and out of Ireland.

The scale and sophistication of the technology which NSA and GCHQ bring to tapping the communications of other states around the world – allies as well as adversaries – is awesome almost beyond imagining.

With their worldwide network of listening posts, computers, antennas, relay stations and spy satellites, the electronic spies and their controlling governments severely compromise the ability of small nations such as Ireland to act effectively in the international political and economic arena. Britain's GCHQ, for example, eavesdrops on the internal negotiating discussions of its EEC 'partners', while the American NSA has woven a tangled communications web around Ireland which ensures that no telephone calls or telexes may pass in or out without in turn passing through its attentive hands.

The spy business, like much else, is being automated, its foot-soldiers a threatened workforce. In the succint words of one commentator, quoting the name of espionage novelist John Le Carré's most celebrated spy-master: 'Exit Smiley, enter IBM'.

One thing is certain: vigilence remains the price of liberty, and in the times which lie ahead we will need to exercise much of the former if the latter is to be protected and enjoyed.

Part I: A Tap on the Line

Introduction

'There is in all states a security system whereby telephones and other communcations are intercepted. It applies in this country as well as others.'[1] These are the words of former Fianna Fáil Taoiseach, Jack Lynch, speaking to the Dáil in May 1970. Lynch's statement was and remains correct: phone-tapping does indeed take place in Ireland. But aside from such simple admissions, few other details about phone-tapping have ever been revealed in the statements of successive government politicians: details such as how many phones are tapped at any particular time and which precise statutory power – if any – legitimises surveillance of this type. Invariably, Dáil exchanges on phone-taps speedily degenerate into slagging matches, with cries of, 'You did it too' being hurled back and forth across the chamber.

For example, when in February 1980, Donegal Fine Gael TD, Paddy Harte, raised allegations of political misuse of phone-tapping, the reply from Fianna Fáil Justice Minister, Gerry Collins, was as evasive as it was humorous: 'God knows, I find it hard enough to listen to what Deputy Harte has to say publicly, let alone what he has to say privately.'[2] It is quite easy to imagine the roles in this particular exchange reversed, as it would be in many of the other similar debates which have taken place down through the years. Either way, whoever is in power and whoever is in opposition, little of what really goes on in the shadowy world of telephone surveillance is ever vouchsafed to the public outside Dáil Éireann.

As a result, it is difficult for the public at large to form a judgement on whether telephone-tapping is a good or bad thing, whether there is too much of it going on or too little. Few – certainly not this author – would hold the view that the right to privacy is absolute and the state should have no authority under any circumstances to intercept phone conversations; even of those engaged in serious crime, in violent subversion or in espionage activities.

Much of this confusion arises from the fact that the public is permitted to know very little if anything about phone surveillance and that the whole practice is shrouded in a cloak of secrecy. To an extent, this makes practical sense. Telephone-tapping is really only of use against the careless and the stupid, which all of us are liable to be at some times. The less people know of how much surveillance is going on, then the more likely they will be to reveal criminal acts over the phone; alternatively, they may assume that all phones are tapped and, in consequence, be driven to less convenient ways of communicating with each other.

Were it shown that those responsible for, and involved in, telephone surveillance had at all times carried out their duties properly and with due regard for the right to privacy of innocent citizens, then one would be willing to leave the phone spies to their headphones, their tape recorders and their discreet visits to telephone exchanges. However, the repeated misuse of authority, the continuing scandals down through the years and the threat posed by new types of mass surveillance technology, all demand that telephone-tapping becomes an issue requiring both public concern and political action.

The most recent episode which raised questions over the use and abuse of phone-taps took place under the Fianna Fáil government of Charles Haughey in 1982, when the telephones of two journalists were tapped by the then Justice Minister, Seán Doherty. Within a month of the Haughey government coming to power in February of that year, Doherty held a lengthy meeting with Assistant Garda Commissioner, Joe Ainsworth, on the subject of press leaks. Doherty expressed disquiet at the amount of government information – even details of cabinet meetings – which was finding its way into the media; in particular, Doherty was worried about journalist Bruce Arnold. On 10 May, Doherty had Arnold's telephone tapped; it remained under surveillance for a further eight weeks until 12 July.

Two weeks later, the phone of another journalist, Geraldine Kennedy was tapped. Kennedy was the first to write about the moves within Fianna Fáil to displace Charles Haughey from the party leadership after the previous general election and had reported closely on the continuing activities of the so-called dissidents. Her telephone conversations were monitored for a period of fourteen weeks, until surveillance ended on 16 November, a week before the second general election of 1982, an election which returned the Coalition parties to power.

Depending on one's point of view, the tapping of Arnold's and Kennedy's telephone conversations was either a flagrant breach of the right of privacy of two guiltless citizens for the purposes of party political advantage; or, alternatively, an entirely necessary and justifiable step, taken to protect the inviolable secrecy of cabinet meetings.

One Fianna Fáil claim, voiced repeatedly during the affair, was that many of those Fine Gael and Labour politicians who were quick to denounce the actions of Haughey and his Minister for Justice, were members in the Coalition government of 1973-77. A government which the Fianna Fáilers alleged, had tapped more telephone conversations than any other, before or since. This was an exaggeration, but it was not a great one. And it was only part of the truth. Telephones had been tapped in Ireland long before that.

Listening to History

Phone-tapping arrived in Ireland with the introduction of the telephone system itself.[3] It is believed that when the country's first exchange opened at Dame Street in Dublin during the 1880s, one of the telephonists' duties was to pass on details of any subversive-sounding conversations to the detectives in G-Division of the Dublin Metropolitan Police, who were based at nearby Dublin Castle. The G-men (a term later adopted by American detectives) worked closely with the Irish Special Branch, controlled by Scotland Yard, and with Military Intelligence, which took its orders from the War Office in London. Certainly the G-men and their associates were not strangers to communications' spying: at that time they operated an elaborate letter-opening system, the origins of which could be traced back to Penal Law days.

When in 1900 the National Telephone Company began operating the Crown Alley exchange off Fleet Street, the G-men set up eavesdropping facilities there and a small team of officers was placed in charge of monitoring telephone conversations. Dublin Castle was thus no longer dependent upon a supply of overheard snippets from telephonists. Phone-tapping, in the full sense of the word, had now arrived.

As the rising tide of militant nationalism began to spread across the country, so too did the tentacles of the phone-tappers. In 1909, K Company of the British Army's Royal Engineers took over the embryonic telecommunications system throughout Leinster, Munster and Connaught, and over the subsequent five years organised telephone and telegraph intercepts for Dublin Castle. Responsibility for phone-tapping was returned to the post office service with the coming of the Great War in 1914. For the next thirty years or so, the Crown Alley exchange in the centre of Dublin remained the nerve centre of all such operations.

Ironically, it was there that spies working for IRA leader Michael Collins intercepted messages to and from Dublin Castle during the Anglo-Irish War of 1918-22. In his autobiography, the Director of British Intelligence in Ireland at the time, Sir Ormond Winter, paid grudging tribute to the espionage successes of Collins and his agents.

The winning of independence in 1921, with the signing of the Anglo-Irish Treaty and the establishment of the twenty-six county Free State, brought with it the need to set up an Irish police force and opportunity to create for the fledgling democracy a new system of legal justice and civil liberties. 'Dublin Castle has fallen,' Michael Collins exclaimed in 1922, 'and with it will have gone all the bureaucratic regulations and tyrannies the people of Ireland suffered under the British regime.' But it was not to be. Two years later, the Cumann na Gaedheal government reproduced those same 'bureaucratic relations' which Collins had decried. In the words of Section 19 of the Garda Síochána Act, 1924: 'Every mention or reference to the Royal Irish Constabulary. . . contained in any statute or statutory rule, order or regulation in force in Saorstát Éireann immediately after the passing of this Act shall be construed and take effect as a mention of or reference to the Garda Síochána.'

Two years later again, an Adaption Order made by the Executive Council transferred to the office of the Minister for Justice the authority to issue postal and telegram interception warrants; previously, this authority had rested with the Lord Lieutenant, under the 1908 Post Office Act. Just as the legislative system surrounding phone taps changed hands unaltered, so too did the physical interception apparatus: Crown Alley continued to tap telephones; only the identity of those under surveillance had changed. The tapping system received a considerable boost in terms of equipment and police manpower during the 1930s, under Garda Commissioner, Eamonn Broy. A room was set aside in Crown Alley and a garda detective was seconded from the Special Branch and placed in charge of eavesdropping operations. As a former member of Michael Collins' espionage network, Commissioner Broy well understood the value of such intelligence-gathering techniques.

The outbreak of the Second World War and the necessity for neutral Ireland to maintain a close watch on the representatives here of belligerent foreign powers presented the country's security and intelligence services with a formidable task. Irish Army Intelligence, G2, and the garda counter-espionage section, C3, proved themselves more than equal to the challenge. The German Legation in Dublin's Northumberland Road was kept under total surveillance: its letters opened and examined; its short-wave radio transmissions monitored and its telephones tapped at Crown Alley.

In 1944, a delegation arrived from the American Office of Strategic Services (OSS), forerunners of the CIA, seeking assurance themselves that information regarding D-Day preparations would not be leaked via Dublin to the Germans. The Americans were uneasy about reports filed by their excitable ambassador in Dublin, David Gray, suggesting widespread support for the Nazis in Ireland. In one particular report, dispatched by Ambassador Gray to President Roosevelt in February 1942, Gray alleged that the Secretary of the Irish Department of External Affairs, Joseph P. Walshe, was leading a group of Nazi sympathisers who were supposedly organised to set up a quisling government in Ireland. The source of Gray's extraordinary claim was none other than the late British Prime Minister, Arthur Balfour, summonded up by Gray in a seance.[4]

The visiting American intelligence officers met with G2 and enquired of its chief, Colonel Dan Bryan, if the telephones at the German Legation were tapped. Colonel Bryan only replied that such an act would constitute a violation of

German sovereignty. Noting that the G2 chief had not actually denied such precautions had been taken, the OSS men assumed – correctly – that the German legation was indeed tapped. If they had also assumed that G2 was tapping the British Embassy, they would have again been correct. Apparently, the phones of the American Embassy were not under surveillance. Perhaps G2 regarded it as unnecessary: they already had a reliable agent placed inside the same embassy.[5]

After the war, the authorities decided to move the tapping centre from the Crown Alley exchange, where it had functioned successively under British and Irish control for over forty years. The Crown Alley exchange still exists to this day and is now one of the more than a dozen switching centres in Telecom Éireann's Dublin city telephone network. A new home for the tappers was found in rooms adjoining a Department of Post and Telegraphs' office, located over a shop in O'Connell Street. There the phone spies would remain for more than three decades.

One of those on the tapping watch-list in those years was Jim Larkin, long-time trade union leader and labour activist. Larkin discovered that his telephone conversations were being monitored when, as a member of the 1947-52 Coalition government, he was able to inspect surveillance files in the Department of Justice. He also learned that many of his comrades in the labour movement were similarly tapped. General Seán MacEoin, the Minister for Justice in that government, remarked many years later that he was amazed at the amount of phone-tapping which was taking place at that time and at the identities of those whose conversations were being monitored.

During the 1950s, telephone engineers themselves began to indulge in some freelance phone-tapping. One who worked at several exchanges in Dublin city later recalled how he and his co-workers whiled away idle moments by eavesdropping

on conversations between a senior civil servant and his
mistress. The fascination of these telephonic intimacies lay
less in any voyeurism than in the fact that the civil servant
would regularly rehearse his minister's forthcoming speeches
with the lady on the other end. Armed with these exclusive
previews of government policy, the telephone engineers
would then dazzle their colleagues with their apparently
psychic knowledge of current affairs.

The targets of more conventional phone-tapping at the
engineer's exchanges during those years included a
businessman suspected of currency irregularities, two ship-
ping lines and a member of the IRA army council.

The phone-tappers hit the headlines in April 1964, when
the British *Sunday Telegraph* newspaper published an article
alleging that telephone surveillance was widespread in Ireland and that the system was abused by goverment politicians. While they could hardly have been pleased by such
media interest in their activities, the phone spies above the
O'Connell Street shop found one small consolation: the *Sunday Telegraph* had got their address wrong. It erroneously
identified the long-vacated Crown Alley exchange as the
nerve centre of phone surveillance.

Predictably, when the newspaper allegations were raised
in the Dáil, it was by a Labour TD, Seán Dunne: those on the
Left of the political spectrum in Ireland have always been
subjected to a disproportionate share of political surveillance. Dunne was assured by the then Fianna Fáil Minister
for Justice, Charles Haughey, that phone intercept warrants
were reviewed at regular intervals and were not kept in force
'unless the need for them was positively established.' Mr
Haughey stressed that 'We are only dealing with criminals. . .
law abiding citizens are outside the scope of this debate. . .
Unless you are known to be engaged in serious crime we have
no interest whatsoever in your telephone conversations.' But
the Labour TD continued to badger Mr Haughey, claiming

that phone-tapping had a dubious legal and constitutional basis, and that its loosely regulated nature left it open to abuse.

Mr Haughey shot back with an attack on 'pseudo-liberals' and defended phone-tapping as a vital instrument in the fight against crime and vice – as distinct from political subversion. 'I wish the Labour Party and those fringe elements would make up their minds and let me know where they stand on matters of this sort. One day they pretend to be enormously perturbed about lawlessness, vice, unsolved crimes and so on, and berate me and the gardaí for not stamping out this or that particular evil. As soon, however, as we take positive action in one direction or another they suddenly discover that they have the most tender conscience and they weep for the poor unfortunate criminal.'

It was during this debate that Mr Haughey made his joking dismissive remark, echoed over a decade later by another Fianna Fáil Justice Minister, Gerry Collins, that phone-tapping was 'the Loch Ness monster of journalism'. If phone-tapping was a monster, it was certainly not a mythical one – and it was a monster which was to return and haunt Haughey during the Arms Crisis and the Arnold/Kennedy affair.

The rising tide of aggressive social and economic protest during the 1960s brought with it an accompanying increase in telephone surveillance. Among those who complained of tapping was militant National Farmers Association leader, Rickard Deasy. High-ranking trade unionists such as Michael Mullin of the Irish Transport and General Workers Union had their telephone conversations tapped. So too had senior members of the Labour Party, including at least one of that party's Dáil representatives, Dr David Thornley. The Earlsfort Terrace offices of the party were also tapped. In addition, the phone spies kept a close watch on the increasing shows of industrial militancy. It was towards the end of this decade that the practice of tapping phones of trade unionists engaged in large-scale strikes became a regular feature of government industrial relations policy. It was a practice which met with some opposition, however. In one episode in 1969, sympathetic telephone exchange engineers in a large provincial city removed tapping connections which the Special Branch had placed on strikers' phones; the taps were not replaced.

As the phone-tapping beast continued to grow and grow, it seemed only a matter of time before it would turn on and ensnare its political masters. And so it happened. During the Arms Crisis of 1970, three government ministers – Charles Haughey, Neil Blaney and Kevin Boland – had their telephones tapped. So too did an army intelligence officer, Captain James Kelly. Kevin Boland's telephone proved somewhat difficult to tap, as there were insufficient spare junction lines to carry his intercepted conversations from his local exchange to the room over the O'Connell Street shop; a solution was eventually found by cutting off other unfortunate subscribers wired to the same exchange.

As widespread as phone-tapping was at the turn of the 1970s, it was only a small foretaste of what was to follow later that decade. A sizeable sum from the £175m Telephone Capital Bill of 1973 was diverted into the secret world of the phone spies. Whether he knew it or not, the Minister for Posts and Telegraphs of the incoming Coalition government, presided over what might be termed as the 'great leap forward' in telephone surveillance in Ireland. When the effects of the 1973 cash injection were being felt by Dublin subscribers, with the opening of a new exchange at Crown Alley and the linking of exchanges at other parts of the city in December 1976, the phone spies were adjusting to the use of new, sophisticated equipment which had been fitted into a room on the top floor of the GPO building. The transition marked the beginning of a new era in large-scale telephone surveillance; it also meant the tappers bidding farewell to their premises above the shop, as they moved across O'Connell Street to their new home.

It is said that more telephones were tapped during the 1973-77 period of the Coalition government that at any other time in the history of the state, before or since. This huge expansion resulted from the convergence of two factors: the obsessive pre-occupation of the Coalition government with subversion and the threat of it; and the availability of new, micro-processor-controlled surveillance equipment, which enabled large numbers of telephones to be tapped at any one time.

Ironically, one item purchased during those years, a multi-track tape recording device, was originally intended to go to a country which was training and funding IRA paramilitaries. The device was manufactured by a British firm as part of a batch of electronic surveillance equipment destined for export to Libya. On learning of the deal, the British authorities ordered the manufacturers to cancel their contract with the Libyans. The gardaí subsequently acquired the device – and at a knock-down price.

Sinn Féin members and other Republican activists were on the receiving end of much telephone interception during that period, as they had been before and since. But so did leading members of the Local Government and Public Services Union, the Dublin Council of Trade Unions, the Irish Transport and General Workers Union and the Association of University Teachers. Activists in pressure groups like the Irish Council of Civil Liberties and the Prisoners Rights' Organisation also came in for surveillance; as did a small local group campaigning against pollution from the American asbestos factory in Ovens, County Cork. Others on the watch-lists included members of the Workers' Party, plus an array of politicians, clergymen and lawyers. Even high-ranking garda officers had taps on their home phones during that heady period.

It should be stressed that not all these phones were tapped at the same time, nor were they under permanent surveillance. A lot depended upon how active or how politically troublesome the targets were perceived to be at any given time. It is believed that most taps of this kind were conducted for fourteen-day periods and were not generally repeated. Journalists, however, attracted more regular attention. Several were warned by their garda contacts or by telephone engineers that their phone conversations were under surveillance. Some contacts pleaded not to be telephoned from the journalists' home phones. Reporters working for the *Irish Times*, the *Irish Independent* and the *Irish Press* newspapers, for *Hibernia* and *Magill* magazines, and for RTE were among the subjects of such scrutiny.[6]

The arrival of the 1977-81 Fianna Fáil administration brought some diminution in phone-tapping. One journalist on a national newspaper assumed he had been taken off the watch-list when his garda contacts were willing to speak freely to him on his home telephone. Yet, by and large, the pattern of widespread surveillance set during the 1973-77 period persisted through the new Fianna Fáil government and through the various administrations which followed it up to the present day.

Striking trade unionists continued to attract the attention of the phone spies, as shown in the 1980 petrol drivers' strike, when two strike leaders had their telephone conversations monitored by the Special Branch. Nor was there any let-up in the closely-guarded secrecy with which the eavesdroppers shrouded their activities. One telephone engineer, who in early 1981 leaked details about tapping to an *Irish Times* journalist, was visited by members of the Special Branch and invited to desist from any such activities in the future. The welfare of his family and his continued state employment were among the factors he was urged to take into consideration.[7]

If telephone surveillance has had its questionable uses in recent years then it has also proved its worth in combating serious crime, at least in kidnap cases. It was a tap on a line at the Enniskerry telephone exchange in County Wicklow in January of 1983 which closed the net on the gang who kidnapped Bray solicitor Bill Somerville. In December of the following year, a routine special Special Branch tap on a phone line between IRA sympathisers in Counties Kerry and Cavan helped to pinpoint the area where the IRA were holding another kidnap victim, supermarket executive, Don Tidey.[8]

The Tappers

Official telephone-tapping in Ireland is a rigorously controlled and strictly supervised business. Only in cases of serious crime or subversion do the various security agencies request the surveillance of telephone lines and, even in these instances, taps are only conducted if the necessary information cannot be obtained in any other fashion. All tapping requests are carefully scrutinised by officials in the Department of Justice and only authorised if the Minister gives consent. All issued warrants are regularly reviewed; and if phone taps are not proving successful, they are immediately removed.

That, in summary, is how the system of telephone-tapping is supposed to operate. The reality is far different. In practice warrants for phone taps are often authorised by Department of Justice officials and are never seen by ministers. Some warrants cover not named individuals, but whole organisations or general lines of garda inquiry – a virtually unlimited category. In addition, many phones are tapped without any form of warrant or authorisation, thanks to a cosy arrangement between Telecom Éireann and the gardaí. In other words, the system does not work, has not worked in the past and unless remedied will continue to lend itself readily to abuse in the future.

In theory, there exist six separate steps or stages in the operation of a telephone tap. Stage one begins with a request for phone surveillance from one of the state agencies responsible for security, among them, the Garda Intelligence and Security Branch (ISB) and the Army Intelligence Unit, which deal with 'political crime', the Garda Central Detective Unit and the Drug Squad, which deal with 'ordinary' crime, and the Investigation Section of the Revenue Commissioners, whose concerns are self-explanatory. In stage two, these requests are examined by Department of Justice officials. If approved, the relevant tapping warrants are personally signed by the Minister for Justice.

The warrants and instructions for tapping the specified telephones are passed on to the Investigation Service of Telecom Éireann in stage three. Formerly known as the Investigation Branch, its members are still referred to in whispers as the 'IB men' by other telephone staff. From a seven man team in the middle 1970s the IB men has grown to include a dozen investigation officers and an unknown number of general staff who are based at Lyon House, a white and black office block on the corner of O'Connell and Cathal Brugha streets in the centre of Dublin. The bulk of the IB men's work is taken up in the investigation of fraud, theft and other crimes committed by telephone staff. Its other role is to liaise with the gardaí in carrying out tapping warrants.[9]

Once the taps are in place, stage four commences with the recording of conversations by telephone engineers on the top floor of the GPO. In stage five, the relevant tapes are brought to garda headquarters in the Phoenix Park and there transcribed on to paper by members of the Investigation and Security Branch. Stage six completes the process, with the transcribed, tapped phone conversations passed to the state agency which requested the surveillance in the first instance – the Drug Squad, Army Intelligence, the Tax Office or whoever.

How closely does this official procedure resemble what actually takes place in the real world? Not very much. In the first place, Ministers for Justice have been known to initiate telephone taps. The surveillance of journalists Bruce Arnold and Geraldine Kennedy is one such example. In their case, the tapping operation was set in motion not by the profess-ional security agencies of the state, but by the Fianna Fáil Justice Minister Seán Doherty.

Secondly, not every warrant is personally signed by the Minister. A 'departmental' signature – that is, by a civil ser-vant, also appears to suffice. Thus, if a prudent Minister wishes to conduct surveillance on a political opponent, he can vaguely hint to his Department that he would not in prin-ciple oppose such a course of action and leave the rest to the officials. Should the affair ever become public the Minister can then truthfully deny that he ever authorised the tapping to take place.

No figures have ever been published showing the number of phone-tapping warrants issued. Speaking in the Dáil in 1980, Fianna Fáil Justice Minister Gerry Collins stated that 'it would not be in the public interest to disclose information regarding the number of warrants in force at any particular time'. Even in the unlikely event of such statistics being made public they would not accurately reflect the actual scale of phone-tapping. This is because many warrants are for whole organisations, or general lines of garda inquiry. In the words of one senior garda officer '. . . it has to be accepted that the phones of innocent people not associated with crime or sub-version will be tapped. . . You could find out more about crime by tapping the phone of a parish priest than you would from the phone of a criminal.'[10]

The above would be cause enough for concern were there not an even greater loop-hole in the operation of the tele-phone-tapping system. *Magill* magazine[11] revealed a friendly understanding existing between the gardaí and Telecom

Éireann whereby lines could be intercepted without any need for a warrant. The tapping centre on the top floor of the GPO is located side by side with what is known as the Service Observation section of Telecom Éireann. In this section, telephone lines around the country are randomly selected for quality analysis. No one using these telephone lines will ever know that every word and sound is carefully scrutinised by Telecom staff. The selected lines vary from week to week. However, with a 'friendly nod' from Telecom Éireann, according to *Magill*, the gardaí are able to request that certain lines are chosen for service observation and all conversations monitored.

Government ministers abusing their positions, over-zealous security chiefs tapping here, there and everywhere, vague and virtually all-embracing powers of surveillance – the picture painted is hardly one of a disciplined system, carefully attentive to the rights of the private citizen. Yet, even if the various procedural stages associated with phone-tapping were adhered to rigorously, it would still remain unclear if the practice had any legal basis at all.

Before exploring this issue, it may be instructive to examine how telephone-tapping is carried out – and more importantly, how new computerised systems carry the potential to make mass telephone surveillance technically achievable, bringing with it the prospect of a 'Big Brother'-type state. If irregularities in the past have failed in galvanising public opinion and in compelling politicians to control electronic surveillance, then a view of what may lie around the corner just might.

Tapping Technology

How are telephones tapped? Where is it done? And by whom? Is there any way of knowing if a particular telephone is under surveillance? If a phone is tapped, will the caller hear strange noises on the line? Is tapping becoming more technically sophisticated? How long will it be before the eavesdroppers will be able to listen to virtually every conversation, thanks to sophisticated computer equipment? These are some of the questions that have arisen in the debate over telephone-tapping. Let us begin by answering the first one.

Technically, a telephone conversation can be tapped at virtually any point along the link from subscriber to subscriber. In practice, official phone-tapping invariably takes place at the local exchange of the targeted individual, where access is easy and detection unlikely. There are some seventeen such exchanges in the Dublin area, plus twenty or so group exchanges around the country. In the majority of these exchanges, large cables enter from the road or street, and spray out on to distribution frames and are connected to long racks of switching equipment.[12]

Behind these distribution frames are devices known to telephone technicians as tapping relays. A particular phone can be tapped by connecting a pair of wires, called a double-jumper, from the targeted line to these relays; from there the tapped line is routed via spare inter-exchange lines to a pre-arranged listening post. Normally, the double-jumpers are attached outside with special master keys. Most telephone staff hold mixed views about the practice. Some have taken to independently checking out distribution frames for connections not listed in the local exchanges, thus identifying the tappers' victims.

A special buffer device, known as a transmission bridge, is always used to ensure that no clicks or other tell-tale noises from the tapping equipment intrude on to an intercepted line; and, as this equipment is not fitted with microphones, it is never possible for the tappers' voices to be heard. In fact tapped lines are usually kept interference free as the eavesdroppers like to be sure that nothing, including background noise and conversations, goes unheard.

In the past, the long hours spent listening to intercepted phone conversations and the tedious sorting of trivial from important traffic, made telephone-tapping a time-consuming and labour intensive practice. This served as a restraint on its extent as tapping operations required a one-to-one ratio of eavesdropper to intercepted line. Now all that has changed, and radically so. Sophisticated monitoring equipment of the type currently used – including computerised multi-track tape recorders and voice recognition systems — enable a mere handful of tappers to maintain surveillance on more than a hundred lines at any one time. One such piece of equipment now used is the Racal International Communications Recorder (ICR). The ICR can record conversations on one hundred and twenty lines simultaneously. Each reel of one inch wide tape is designed to store twenty-four hours of intercepted traffic; and when one reel reaches its end, another is automatically switched on, thus enabling continuous, round-the-clock surveillance. A sister device used with the ICR is the Racal Timesearch unit. Timesearch can scan multi-track tapes at six hundred times the recording speed, taking just over two minutes to examine the entire contents of a full, twenty-four hour tape. It picks out the digital codes placed there when the recording was made. These codes indicate the number of the phone on which the call was made, the number dialled, the duration of the call. If, for example, one wanted to replay any calls made by A to B and C, but not to anyone else, then the Racal Timesearch unit can be programmed to extract these from a twenty-four hour tape in a matter of seconds.

The Key Executive Safeguard (KES) ATR 5 system is also used. This KES device can monitor fifty phone lines at any one time. It can be programmed to record only at a certain time of day on a selected line, or on a particular day of the week. It can even be programmed to record phone calls only when a specified voice is heard on the line. This last facility was developed by KES engineers in co-operation with British Telecom, and is widely used by the security services in Britain.

Despite all this high-tech sophistication, things do occasionally go awry for the phone-tappers. Sometimes it is the tape recorders that cause problems. The disturbing experience of one *Irish Times* journalist provides a case in point. After a lengthy conversation with a senior politician, the journalist replaced the receiver and then picked it up again to make another call – only to hear the previous conversation being played back on the line! This phenomenon is not unknown in Britain, either. Joan Ruddock, the Chairwoman of the Campaign for Nuclear Disarmament (CND), has complained of hearing her own private conversations played back on her telephone line.

One of the more risible foul-ups in recent times for the phone-tappers also occurred in Britain. During the 1970s the Security Services (MI5) developed the key-word recognition system which was designed to operate in conjunction with the tape-recorders used in phone-tapping; by only monitoring conversations which contain specified key-words – for example, 'protest', 'nuclear' or whatever – the tappers hoped to automate the whole laborious process of sorting out interesting conversations from unimportant ones. Unfortunately one of the key words was 'strike', and during the miners strike of 1984, the eavesdropping system was sent into almost total disarray as virtually every second telephone conversation contained some reference to the strike.

Yet it would be foolish indeed to dismiss the increasing sophistication of the phone-tappers and their equipment. The technology to enable mass telephone interception to become a reality is a lot closer than is generally thought and this prospect makes it all the more vital that strict contols are placed on the use of state surveillance.

Yes – But Is It Legal?

Despite the extensive proportions which phone-tapping has assumed, and for all the hi-tech sophistication of its practitioners no court in the Republic has ever had state evidence submitted to it which was based explicitly upon intercepted telephone conversations. Two conclusions follow directly from this. Either no operationally valuable or legally incriminating information has ever been so obtained by the security authorities and the whole business has been a complete waste of time.

Or – more plausibly – the state has been consistently unwilling to place its telephone-tapping powers before any legal test. And with good reason. For prior to the proposed Interception of Postal Packets and Telecommunications Messages Bill, published by the Coalition government in December 1985, no law has been introduced – let alone enacted – to authorise telephone surveillance, with or without a warrant. Furthermore, there was every reason to believe that the loosely regulated nature of the practice here was in clear breach of the European Convention on Human Rights.

With bizarre logic, the piece of legislation most frequently and most solemnly advanced by successive government ministers in defence of the state's supposed right to eavesdrop on the private phone conversations of its citizens predates Alexander Graham Bell's invention of the telephone by over a century and a half. This is the Post Office (Revenue) Act, passed by the House of Commons in 1710. Section 40 of this Act recognised the authority of Post Office personnel to open and inspect letters and other mails, subject to a warrant from the Lord Lieutenant.[13]

Then 1710 Act regularised powers already conferred upon the Post Office by two earlier Crown Proclamations; one,

issued by Queen Elizabeth in 1591, authorised the seizing of
mails coming into Ireland from abroad; and a second, dated
1626, extended that right to items posted within the country.
It is instructive to note that one of the reasons cited in 1657
for the establishment of a crown monopoly of the Post Office
service was to with greater effect 'discover and prevent many
dangerous and wicked designs which had been and are daily
contrived against the peace and welfare of the Common-
wealth.'

Section 40 of the 1710 Post Office (Revenue) Act remained
in force for almost two hundred years. It passed materially
unchanged through Section 25 of the Post Office (Offences)
Act, 1837, reaching its final destination as Section 56 of the
Post Office Act, 1908. A subsequent adaption order made in
July 1926 by the President of the Free State Executive Council
transferred to the new office of the Minister for Justice the
power to issue postal interception warrants previously held
by the Lord Lieutenant. It was this 1908 Act which was used
by Ministers for Justice Charles Haughey and Des O'Malley
in 1966 and 1972, and by Taoiseach Jack Lynch in 1969, when
claiming that the state was empowered to issue telephone
surveillance warrants.

It did nothing of the sort. Section 56 of the 1908 Post Office
Act did recognise the authority of Post Office staff to carry
out the 'opening. . . detaining or delaying of a postal packet'
– an authority conferred centuries previously by Crown Proclamations. The Act explicitly defined a 'postal packet' as a
'letter, postcard, newspaper, packet, pattern or sample packet
and every pack or article transmissable by post and includes
a telegram.' No mention of telephones is to be found or of
any ministerial authority to interfere with conversations
carried thereby.

Not surprisingly, the 1908 Act was quietly forgotten in
justifying phone-taps. In more recent years, the line changed
and ministers have sought refuge in a different – but even

less relevant – piece of legislation. Quizzed on the subject of telephone surveillance in September 1980, Fianna Fáil Justice Minister Gerry Collins told the Dáil that he was empowered to issue such warrants under the Wireless Telegraphy Act of 1926. This was complete nonsense.

The 1926 Act confers powers upon the minister – the Minister for Communications at that, and not the Minister for Justice – only in respect of wireless telegraphy; this is specified in the Act as 'any system of communicating messages. . . by means of radiated electro-magnetic waves originating in an apparatus constructed for the purpose of originating such communications.'

Telephone sets are not in any sense constructed for the purpose of originating such radio waves. If they were, Telecom Éireann subscribers would be required, under the same Act, to possess broadcasting licences in the same fashion as RTE. In addition, no ministerial powers to intercept any form of communications, whether radio waves or anything else, are contained in the 1926 Wireless Telegraphy Act. Its purpose is purely administrative and regulatory.

It would appear from all this that from the foundation of the state up to recent times there existed no legislation in Irish law which empowered the Minister for Justice to issue telephone surveillance warrants. But did that make the practice illegal? In answering that question it may be instructive to examine the situation in Britain, as our legislation mirrors that in force there.

In June 1978, James Malone, an antique dealer from Coldharbour in Surrey was in court on charges of handling stolen goods, an offence of which he was later acquitted. In the course of his trial, Malone discovered that a page in the notebook of a testifying police officer contained a transcript of a telephone call which he had made. After an adjournment, counsel for the crown admitted to the court that Malone's telephone was indeed tapped by the police.

Following his acquittal on the stolen goods charges, Malone brought a private action against the crown. He alleged that the tapping of his telephone was not lawful under British law; that it breached the privacy of communications provisions in the European Convention on Human Rights; and that there existed a further breach in the European Convention in that he had no means of redress against the Crown for this interference in his privacy.

At the end of the Malone court case, the judge, Vice-Chancellor Sir Robert Megarry, gave a seventy-three page reserved judgement which took two hours, ten minutes to deliver. He said that the phone-tapping system in Britain was not one in which 'it is possible to feel any pride in English law' and that 'it cries out for legislation.' However, Sir Robert ruled that, although telephone surveillance was not explicitly authorised in British law, it was not prohibited either. So, strictly speaking, no offence had been committed against Malone. It is reasonable to assume that Ireland's phone-tappers, although acting without any explicitly legislative authority, were similarly not breaking any law.

Megarry did stress that the system was so loosely regulated as to make it 'abundantly clear' that British practice would be found unacceptable to the European Court on Human Rights. However, he insisted that the European Convention was not enforceable in British courts.

The relevant provisions in the European Convention are Articles 8 and 13. The former states that 'Everyone has the right to respect for his private and family life, his home and his correspondence. There shall be no interference by a public authority with the exercise of this right except such as in accordance with the law and is necessary in a democratic society in the interests of national security, public safety or the economic well-being of the country, for the prevention of disorder or crime, for the protection of health and morals, or for the protection of the rights and freedoms of others.'

Article 13 states that 'Everyone whose rights and freedoms as set forth in this Convention are violated shall have an effective remedy before a national authority notwithstanding that the violation had been committed by persons acting in an official capacity.'

Malone took his case to Europe and – in August 1984 – he won. In a previous case, that of Klass and others versus the Federal Republic of Germany, the court had ruled in September 1978 that signatory states did not have 'an unlimited discretion to subject persons within their jurisdiction to secret surveillance', that telephone-tapping was acceptable 'under exceptional circumstances'; and that therefore minimum safeguards were necessary to protect the rights of the individual under Article 8 of the European Convention. The court ruled that the West German system satisfied these minimum conditions.

In West Germany, telephone surveillance is covered by legislation and is supervised by a parliamentary committee. In addition, there is a right of complaint against suspected interception and a requirement of notification to the victim once surveillance has ceased.

Malone's victory in the European Court has necessitated the introduction of stricter legislation in Britain in compliance with the Articles 8 and 13 of the Convention. This was the Interception of Communications Bill, which set out the precise circumstances in which the government can authorise the interception of mail and telecommunications: the prevention or detection of serious crime, the safe-guarding of national security and the protection of the economic well-being of the country. It also established a tribunal, headed by a judge, to investigate and remedy alleged abuses of the system.

Sixteen months after Malone's victory in Europe, and three years after the Arnold/Kennedy phone-tapping controversy, Coalition Minister for Justice Michael Noonan published his

Interception of Postal Packets and Telecommunications Act. This sought to bring the practice of telephone surveillance in Ireland to within the conditions laid down by the European Convention. On the face of it, it would do exactly that – if passed into law. It has not; nor is there any indication that it will in the foreseeable future.

It is luminously obvious that any case similar to James Malone's brought by an Irish citizen prior to 1986 would be assured of similar success – provided that the person bringing the case had clear evidence of his or her telephone being subject to official surveillance.

Two Irish citizens who found themselves in this unhappy category were journalists Bruce Arnold and Geraldine Kennedy. Just one week before the European Court gave its verdict in favour of James Malone, Arnold and Kennedy initiated their successful High Court proceedings claiming that their rights under the Irish Contitution had been infringed by taps placed on their telephones by the Fianna Fáil government.

And here rests a crucial point. While the laws under which both the English antique dealer and the Irish journalists were tapped are similar, there remains the crucial difference in that Ireland has a written Constitution with clearly defined rights and liberties, while Britain does not. Arnold and Kennedy alleged that their constitutional right to privacy had been violated. In winning their case they showed that those who ordered their phones to be tapped in 1982 were acting not only without any legal foundation; they were also acting unconstitutionally.

The fact remains that the successive Irish governments and Ministers for Justice had long been responsible for a system of surveillance which contravenes the European Convention on Human Rights. This delay in implementing proper phone-tapping legislation, and its somewhat forced arrival due to external obligations, cannot but invite the perception that it was not any desultoriness which for so long restrained

successive Irish legislators; rather, the deliberate unwillingness to forfeit such a convenient, tried and tested weapon
against opponents within the political establishment and
against the politically troublesome on the outside.

Part II: A Bug in the Room

Introduction

Every day businesses everywhere lose large amounts of money through lack of internal security. Petty pilfering, theft, information and contract losses are among the more common problems which at the least can lead to drastically reduced profits and at the worst can result in liquidation or bankruptcy. Unfortunately the conscientious businessman or woman cannot rely simply on increased vigilance on his or her part and regard must be paid to securing a business internally as well as externally.

Electronic surveillance equipment represents a highly effective and efficient aid to keeping a finger on the pulse of your business operation whilst also enabling any 'bad apples' to be quickly and quietly filtered out. Whatever the size of your business from one man to a corporation you will benefit from the insight that covert surveillance can offer.

The above is a quote from publicity literature issued by a British manufacturer of bugging and other electronic snooping devices. Bugs are significant tools in the world of intelligence-gathering. Private detectives use them to pry out business and company secrets, and governments rely increasingly on them to monitor criminals and political dissidents. How great is the extent of bugging in this country? Are bugs widely used by private eyes and by the gardaí? How exactly do such devices work? Is there sufficient grounds for introducing legislation to regulate their usage? It is with these questions that the following chapters deal.

Here, There and Everywhere

When the forty employees at a Dublin machine-hire depot reported for work on the morning of 7 June 1978, they had no way of knowing what extraordinary events waited in store for them. Before that day would be out, they were to find themselves at the centre of the most bizarre dispute ever to feature in the history of Irish industrial relations. Within hours of arriving at the office, the staff would be halting all work, holding an emergency union meeting and angrily storming out of their employer's premises.

Three days passed before a union-company settlement was arrived at. Had the dispute been caused by differences over pay or work conditions, there would have been little to set it apart from the dozens of others which occurred that year. But this dispute was different: the company was bugging its workers and had been caught doing it!

The bizarre events of that Wednesday began in the building's radio control room, from where instructions were broadcast to lorry drivers on the road. Feeling a little cold in the room, one of the operators tried to start up an old, disused electric heater, only to notice a strong burning smell emanating from it. Having removed the heater's cover, the operator found a small electronic device, about the size of a matchbox. An expert brought in by the employee's union, ITGWU Branch No. 5, confirmed initial suspicions that the device was in fact a bug planted to monitor conversations between operators in the control room.

It was subsequently learned that the bug had been covertly installed on the premises by a private security firm, acting on the advice of a detective from Dublin Castle. Apparently, the company believed its employees were doing 'nixers' on the job, or else were leaking confidential business inform-

ation to rival firms – and had sought underhand means to
verify its suspicions. Following the accidental discovery of
the device and the resulting three-day strike, the company
faithfully promised never to bug its employees again.[14]

The bugging episode did more than upset worker-employer
relations in the company. It showed that the latest and most
devious type of electronic surveillance technology had
reached private individuals in Ireland. Up to the mid 1970s
bugging devices were expensive and complicated pieces of
equipment, little used outside government security services.
The development of the microchip and of miniaturised electronic components changed all that completely. The same
technology that was introducing the pocket calculator and
digital watch was at the same time bringing into circulation
tiny high-powered bugging devices – and at a cost of ten
pounds or less. Bugs were also becoming easier to obtain.
The intending Irish bugger could now readily acquire surveillance devices through mail order from the ten or so British
firms who commercially manufactured such equipment; or
directly over-the-counter, from 'security' equipment shops
in Britain.

Further episodes of employers bugging their workforces
were brought to light by *New Hibernia* magazine.[15] The first
was at a meat plant. Management had hired a Dublin private
detective agency to install an eavesdropping device behind
a twin power socket in the plant's canteen, where employees
held their union meetings. Apparently, the bug was first
placed in September of 1984, for the purpose of spying on a
particularly critical union meeting. It worked so well that the
management decided to leave it in position. Thirteen months
passed before workers discovered the bug, which was connected by a thin cable to a tape recorder in an office used by
a manager. At the time of the bug's discovery in
November 1985, he was absent from the plant.

Also caught in the process of electronically spying on its workers was a company in Dublin. Employees found a telephone tapping device designed to monitor all incoming and outgoing calls hidden in a filing cabinet. The embarrassed management agreed to the demands of the workers' trade union, the ITGWU, that they be permitted every four months to bring in their own private detective who would 'sweep' the factories. The workers could choose the precise time their anti-bugging expert would arrive and management would pay all associated costs.[16]

Another case revealed by *New Hibernia* magazine centred on a factory where a bug was placed by a private detective in the company's offices. This time around it was not a case of management spying on workers; rather the bug was installed at the behest of a rival company, seeking to discover customers, contract prices and other commercial information.[17]

The often stormy field of industrial relations again provided the setting for another bugging case, this time at a County Cork hotel in November 1981. A conference room in the Bantry Bay Hotel was hired for a day by the Employment Appeals Tribunal to hear the case of a man who claimed unfair dismissal from the local division of the Gulf Oil Company. In theory, the Tribunal was sitting in private session; in fact, the proceedings were monitored by a bug hidden inside a television set in a corner of the conference room. The bug was linked by radio signal to a car parked outside in Bantry town square, only a hundred yards away.

When the Tribunal chairperson became aware that the hearing was bugged, proceedings were adjourned. The gardaí were called in, the hotel room searched, the bug located and the occupant of the car outside interviewed by the gardaí. 'I cannot over-stress my revulsion at what has happened,' the Tribunal chairperson told an *Irish Press* reporter, adding that the hearing would not continue until, in the words of Perry Mason, 'the room is cleaned.'

The Bantry eavesdropper was subsequently charged under the 1926 Wireless Telegraphy Act for operating a radio transmitter without a licence from the Minister for Communications. It is the only prosecution to date for electronic snooping; and as we shall see, this 1926 Act is most unsuitable for the prosecution of cases of this kind.[18]

One survey of the ten or so private detective agencies operating in Dublin revealed that most are willing to use bugging devices on behalf of a paying client – but only under certain circumstances. 'You (would) have to prove you are having bad trouble', was how one private eye put it.[19] One thing is certain, their services do not come cheap. The going rate for hiring private detectives in Ireland is twenty pounds an hour upwards, with additional expenses and charges on top of that. Having a bug installed alone can cost a client anywhere in the region of six hundred pounds.

Although concealed microphones and phone-taps are the more spectacular aspects to the work of private detectives, some members of that profession seldom resort to such methods. They prefer to rely instead on the more traditional methods of information-gathering: keeping their eyes and ears open, together with chatting up their target's friends, workmates and neighbours. One Dublin private eye tells of a case in which he succeeded in obtaining confidential details from a minor civil servant regarding an up-and-coming contract his client was after. 'All I had to do after I had targeted him was to listen to an hour of boring conversation about fishing – and buy him three pints of stout.'

'The trouble with most of these James Bond devices you see on TV,' claims one Irish industrial spying expert, 'is that they only work on television. I would use a bug if there was no other way to get information for my client. Apart from the fact that half the time the things don't work properly because they are too near electrical cables in the walls, or because the people you want to listen to are facing the other way, there is the problem of installing them, and keeping them going (with batteries) . . . In most cases that is too much of a risk.'[20]

It is difficult to gauge exactly how much electronic snooping does go on in this country. Certainly, it does take place, and it is by no means limited to the areas of industrial spying between rival companies, or to employer-worker disputes. Bugs have been used in matrimonial cases, which are another steady source of income to the private eye business. One prominent name in the Irish show business world discovered this fact to his cost. Having spent a furtive night with a woman friend in a Dublin private house, he subsequently found himself confronted with a tape recording of the entire performance. It may not have been of any great interest to him, but the bug planted by a private eye was a top of the market model, originally designed for use by the British Security Services, MI5.

The justification claimed by private eyes for using bugging devices – that their clients are under threat from blackmailers, thieves or whatever, to such a serious extent that breaches of privacy are legitimate – would be more convincing if it came from a profession that was tightly controlled and had a reputation for acting with responsibility. Unfortunately, that is not the case in this country. In recent times there have been two cases where private eyes have been convicted of offences — one of them for burglary committed in connection with investigations on behalf of clients. Literally anyone can set up a private detective agency in Ireland, as no system of control or licensing exists. Neither are prospective private eyes vetted for criminal records, a situation that leaves bona fide clients in danger of blackmail or double-crossing.

Politicians and gardaí have for several years called for this chaotic and dangerous situation to be rectified and for some form of licensing to be brought into operation. So too has the

Chairperson of the Association of Irish Investigators (AII), a
voluntary representative body. According to the AII Chairperson, 'with no control on who sets up an agency, certain private
eyes can take short-cuts, and use dubious methods to acquire
information.'[21]

The media, which is often loud in its condemnation of
bugging, phone-tapping and the like, has its own practitioners in the dubious and illegal business of electronic snooping.
One national newspaper has on several occasions hired the
services of a Dublin private detective who freely admits to
using bugging methods. Another newspaper bugged the
chamber of the Dáil during the Finance Minister's budget
speech in 1981. The device used – a walkie talkie type radio
transmitter – was concealed inside the handbag of a lady
journalist. Not only did this innovative — and illegal —
technique enable the paper to steal a march on its competitor,
it also anticipated by three years the authorised live transmissions of budget speeches on RTE radio.[22]

The Good Bug Guide

Bugs and other electronic spying devices are a lot easier to
obtain than most people might imagine. The simplest method
is through mail order. At least two magazines which circulate
in the Republic carry regular advertisements for surveillance
equipment. 'Transistorised transmitters. Unbeatable value.
Receive on domestic VHF/FM radio, coverage 70-150 Mhz. . .
pick up whispers at 20 feet. . . 1 mile range, self-contained

ready for use. £13.50.' So runs one advertisement in a weekly magazine, available from most newsagents throughout the country. Here is another advertisement from the same issue: 'Micro transmitters, telephone devices, surveillance receivers, etc. All guaranteed equipment. Prices from £17.50.' And who could resist this offer? 'Hear every word. FM micro transmitter with microphone or telephone device, listen on any VHF radio, £9.95.' Such advertisements are prefaced with a reminder that 'it is an offence to use transmitting equipment without a Home Office Licence'. The fact that licences for bugging devices have never been, and will never be in the future, issued by the British Home Office – or by our own Department of Communications – seems to be neither here nor there.

Another magazine that features advertisements for electronic surveillance equipment is supported wholly by advertising revenue. This publication is mailed free to many businesses in the Republic. Most advertisements offer conventional office equipment and furnishing – filing cabinets, typewriters, correcting fluids, stationery, etc. However, the executive reader will also find items such as the so-called ATRI5, which 'connects very simply to the telephone line at any point. . . does not need to be anywhere near a phone. Plugs into a cassette recorder and from that point. . . both sides of all phone conversations, either incoming or outgoing will be recorded. . . requires no batteries and can be used with any recorder.' Although the ATRI5 is advertised as a clandestine method of tapping one's own business telephone to discover abuse by employees ('How is your phone used while you are away?') it is obvious that the device would be equally effective in bugging other peoples' telephones. A competing firm, for example, or a rival for internal promotion.

Getting their hands on sophisticated equipment is therefore not likely to be too much of a problem for those who – for whatever reason – intend to use bugging devices. Quite the contrary, the would-be eavesdropper is liable to be spoilt for choice by the range and complexity of devices readily available. A greater headache is probably the selection of the most appropriate bug for the particular job from the bewildering array of gadgetry on offer. What are the technical characteristics of bugging devices that make some more suited to certain operations than others — and what distinguishes high-performance equipment from less reliable, less satisfactory devices?[23]

Essentially, all models of bugs have three defining features or parameters that together determine their suitability for particular eavesdropping operations: size, power source and signal transmission. Because bugs are pre-eminently clandestine devices, compactness and the capability to 'melt' into their intended surroundings are vital. Many bugging devices come in miniature plastic containers about the size of a matchbox. These are well suited to concealment behind radiators or pictures, under desks or tables, in low pressure air conditioning vents and similar places. Alternatively, bugs can be built into the structure of everyday objects – ashtrays, pen stands, cigarette lighters, clocks, etc. – and their presence masked in this manner. Sometimes, bugs need no deceptive packaging. If placed inside telephones, radios or other items of conventional electrical equipment, the average person is unlikely to be able to distinguish one jumble of wires and components from any other.

Power supply is the next problem. The standard matchbox or ashtray model bug, with a transmitting range of four hundred metres or a quarter of a mile, will operate continuously for a duration of five to fifty hours. The exact operating life will vary with the bug's power requirements. After that its miniature batteries, which are similar to those used in digital watches or hearing aids, will need replacement. If the eavesdropper has free access to the bugged premises – it may be his own workplace or home – then battery replacement is unlikely to present too many difficulties. Obvious problems do arise, however, if one is bugging some other person's office or house. The surreptitious – and illegal – entry into the targeted premises for installing the listening device is liable to pose hazards; gaining entry time and time again to replace batteries is likely to be impossible.

Bug manufacturers have developed a number of techniques to deal with the power supply problem. Some stretch the bug's operating life, others eliminate the need for batteries altogether. One of the former techniques is the voice activated microphone, a device that triggers the bug only when it detects conversations taking place. When the triggering sounds cease, the bug will stop transmitting and return to a dormant stand-by condition in which it draws only a tiny amount of battery power. The voice activated bug is ideal for eavesdropping on rooms which are likely to be empty for lengthy periods; if a conventional bug was used, the battery life would be wasted by transmitting silence. In some cases, a voice activated bug can function without the need for battery replacement over periods of several weeks.

Another method of stretching the life of battery powered bugs is to remotely control them through a radio signal. One such model advertised by a British manufacturer can lie dormant for as long as three months on a single battery, waiting for a specially coded radio signal to switch it on to an active surveillance mode. An additional attraction of radio-controlled listening devices is that they reduce the risk of discovery. Most bug-detection devices look for the signal transmitted by bugs and not the actual bugs themselves. So if the eavesdropper suspects that the targeted premises is to be 'swept' for bugs at a particular time, the bug can be shut down by remote radio signal. The individual or organisation concerned will discover nothing and continue in the false assurance that no clandestine surveillance is taking place.

One radio-controlled bug which was discovered, however,

was planted by the British Security Services, MI5, at the London headquarters of the Communist Party in 1975. Builders came across the device while renovating a conference room; it was concealed inside a wooden beam which supported panelling surrounding the platform. The bug was powered by long-life mercury batteries and independent experts judged it to be ten or twelve years old.

Perhaps the most ingenious method of solving the power source problem is to conceal the listening device inside equipment which is itself electrically live. The bugged light bulb is one such example. It may be inserted in a conventional desk lamp or other bulb holder. Fitted with a small transformer, it draws its power from the electric mains. The microphone and transmitter are concealed in the base of the bulb. They will continue to operate as long as the bulb remains plugged into the socket. The bugged light bulb looks indistinguishable from an ordinary bulb and provides illumination in the usual way. Another variation of this method is the wall adaptor bug. From the outside it completely resembles a conventional thirteen amp, three pin, two way adaptor and is fully functional. Inside, however, is a bugging device which cleverly uses the mains supply as a power source and the related earth pin wiring as an effective aerial. 'Sophisticated but simple,' claims the manufacturers of one such adaptor bug in their publicity material. 'The high sensitivity internal microphone can pick up conversations up to 30 feet away and relay them to a VHF/FM radio up to 500 yards away with exceptional clarity. . .' Installation time is absolutely minimum, just plug it in.'

While some bugging devices eliminate reliance on batteries by drawing current from the electric mains, others can get the power they need from conventional radio or television stations. Inside each of these bugs there is what is technically known as a tuned circuit, wired to a storage capacitor. By connecting these to a short aerial, the received signal strength can be sufficient to operate a low-powered bug indefinitely. Radio or television powered bugs are rather bulky, however, and will only work reliably when in the vicinity of a broadcasting station; anywhere reasonably close to an RTE 2 VHF radio transmitter should do nicely.

Once the bug is covertly installed and has a reliable power source, the next problem is some means of relaying the monitored information back to the eavesdropper. Radio transmission is by far the most widely used method, and because the smallest radio transmission aerials are those in the VHF band, micro-miniaturised VHF radio transmitters are the most common radio bugs. The generally practical range is in the region of 50 to 700 Mhz. There is a strong preference for the fringes of the commercial VHF band of 88 to 108 Mhz. This is because most domestic VHF radios can be readily altered to pick up signals on the edges of this band.

Contrary to what might be expected, bugs with a short range of a few hundred metres are more recommended by experts than those which can transmit over a distance of two or three miles. The former variety have less chance of accidental discovery by radio hams, VHF programme listeners, radio taxis – even garda cars with their own radio sets. A British private detective ended up with a nine month jail sentence and a five hundred pound fine in 1971 for bugging offences in London. The bugs had been accidentally picked up by a radio ham who subsequently tipped off the police.[24]

Telephones exercise a great attraction over private detectives and freelance snoopers. Partly because so much information passes over telephone lines bugging them can provide revealing insights into the activities and intentions of persons of interest. And partly because telephones conveniently offer the bugger a free source of electric power (the line voltage), a ready-made microphone (the handset) and an aerial (the phone line itself) which is ideal for boosting the transmitting range of any bug.

A commonly used telephone listening device is the so-called 'drop-in' bug. This is a tiny VHF radio transmitter shaped so as to look indistinguishable from the conventional mouthpiece of a telephone. It would take less than a minute for anyone to unscrew the ordinary mouthpiece and insert the bugged replica, and once installed it will transmit all conversations on that line. If undetected, it will operate indefinitely as no batteries are needed.

The 'drop-in' phone bug requires the eavesdropper to enter the victim's premises. If this is too much of a problem, the 'direct-wire' bug may be more approriate. This method involves attaching a bug via an interface device to the victim's phone line. Alternatively, a tape recorder may be used instead of a bug. Either way, the eavesdropper is provided with a means of monitoring incoming and outgoing calls on the bugged line. Again no batteries are needed.

The advantage of the 'direct-wire' method is that the bug or tape recorder can be linked in at any convenient point between the victim's telephone and the local exchange. A favourite location is the point at which the telephone wire comes on to the public road or street from the targeted office, house, embassy etc. Another convenient bugging site is the victim's local roadside telephone cabinet. According to one newspaper report[25] roadside telephone cabinets are frequently unlocked, or prised open by vandals. Those that are locked will open with a master key; it is known that copies of these keys, which can unlock most telephone cabinets in the Republic, have passed outside official hands.

According to the report, private detectives in Ireland are experts at this type of clandestine bugging. To indentify the line in question from the arrays of wires in the roadside cabinet, the eavesdropper rings the victim's phone and then apologises for dialling the wrong number. After the victim hangs up, the phone spy plays a transistor radio or some other such recognisable sound into the phone from which the call was made. Then, using a do-it-yourself bugging kit, the spy checks all the lines passing through the cabinet until the victim's is identified. He then links the victim's phone line to one in a rented flat in the local area, where the bugged conversations could be monitored on a tape recorder.

Undoubtably the most exotic piece of telephone bugging equipment is the 'infinity transmitter', so called because its inventor claimed it could monitor conversations in a room from anywhere in the world. This is not strictly a bug at all, but a tone-operated switching device attached to the microphone in the handset of the target's telephone. It requires no batteries and does not interfere with the telephone's ordinary performance.

Once the device is installed, an eavesdropper dials the victim's phone number. When it is answered, he apologies for ringing the wrong number. The victim then replaces the handset – but the eavesdropper does not replace his. As the originator of the call must break the connection, the line between the two telephones remains open. However, as the victim has replaced the handset upon the phone cradle, the microphone inside the handset automatically switches off and the eavesdropper cannot hear anything from his end of the line.

This is where the other half of the infinity transmitte comes into play. The eavesdropper activates a tone generator at his end of the line – an electronic bleeper, for example, or even a harmonica played at the right note. The switching device hidden inside the victim's phone recognises the tone and turns the microphone in the handset on again. From then on, the eavesdropper can monitor conversations and sounds in the room where the target telephone is until he decides to hang up his own phone. The clandestine eavesdropping can be carried out any number of times and there are no distance

restrictions. The eavesdropper can plant the bug in the
victim's telephone one day and ring from another continent
weeks later. In the telephone systems of some countries it is
even unnecessary to ring a 'wrong number' – by sending the
right tones down the line in the seconds before the victim's
phone rings, monitoring can take place without the victim
even suspecting that there is anyone at the other end of the
line. 'Infinity transmitters' only work on direct lines, however; the standard PABX internal business exchange defeats
them completely. Paradoxically, some security-minded
executives leave themselves wide open to surveillance of this
kind by insisting upon direct outside lines to their desks,
rather than the more common PABX system.

Because the 'drop-in', 'direct wire' and 'infinity transmitter' bugs all derive electrical power from the telephone
system, they are open to detection by line monitoring equipment of the type used by both Telecom Éireann test engineers
and by private detectives who offer bug-detection services.
In the United States, the voltage and other specifications of
telephone lines are quite exact and clearly defined, so any
departure from these is a reliable indication that something
is amiss. With the older, less sophisticated apparatus used
by Telecom Éireann, line specifications fluctuate considera-
bly, making bug detection a far more difficult operation. Only
very crude or amateur bugs are certain of discovery by line
monitoring equipment – a fact that the suspicious-minded
should remember if ever they hire private detectives to
'sweep' their telephones.

Electronic bugging is illegal. Under the Wireless Telegraphy Act of 1926, no one may initiate any form of radio
transmission without first obtaining a broadcasting licence
from the Minister for Communications. However, the 1926
Act is a rather blunt instrument for tackling the problem of
electronic spying because it was drafted with the administration of national radio services in mind and not the safeguard-

ing of citizens' privacy against the threat of unauthorised bugging. 'We have enough on our plate without going after businessmen who are hiring fellows to steal their rivals' secrets,' an officer at garda headquarters has been quoted as saying. 'We will prosecute if there is a break-in and we get the culprit. We haven't much chance if we go to court to prosecute a man for operating a tiny transmitter with a hidden microphone when there are big pirate radio transmitters operating openly around the country.[26]

For the foreseeable future, it looks very much as if the absence of strict legislation targeted specifically against bugging, the inappropriateness of the 1926 Act, the growing sophistication of spying devices and the virtual certainty of escaping detection, will all combine to ensure that electronic bugging continues unchecked, with an ever lengthening list of victims.

State Bugging

Private eyes are not the only ones who engage in electronic surveillance. Governments, through their security and intelligence agencies, do it as well. The Irish government and the gardaí are certainly no exception. What began almost as a hobby for a garda officer twenty years ago now has a sizeable amount of manpower and resources committed to it. The victims of garda bugging over the past two decades have ranged from suspected murderers, to the IRA to Fianna Fáil leader Charles Haughey. As in the case of telephone-tapping, the legislation surrounding the use of bugging equipment by the gardaí is far from satisfactory.

One of the first bugging operations undertaken by the gardaí was carried out in Munster at the end of the 1960s. The target was a farmer, whom gardaí strongly suspected of involvement in a local murder case. Suspicions were all the gardaí had, however. The farmer had covered his tracks well and had given a faultless performance under interrogation. He was subsequently released and returned to his farmhouse. There he discussed, in graphic terms, details of the murder act with his sister. It was his first and last mistake.

The gardaí had some hours previously broken into the farmhouse and planted a bugging device. Their suspicions fully confirmed and armed with all the details of the crime's commission, the gardaí arrested the farmer and interrogated him again. This time he confessed. The bringing to justice of this murderer must have been particularly satisfying for one of the officers involved in the investigation. An electronics enthusiast, he had previously been attached to the Radio Section at garda headquarters. It was there he developed an interest in bugging devices, almost as a hobby, and had introduced his colleagues to the potential benefits to the garda force of electronic bugging equipment. It was a hobby fast becoming a valuable technique of information gathering.[27]

If this farmhouse bugging was one of the more successful garda operations of its kind, another case of electronic spying which followed shortly afterwards was surely one of the most controversial. Its target was not a common criminal; it was government minister, Charles Haughey. The time was the autumn of 1970 and Mr Haughey, along with others, was facing trial for conspiring to import arms.

During the course of the Arms Trial, Mr Haughey's Malahide home was visited and bugged by the gardaí. Three officers drove up to his home in a Department of Posts and Telegraphs van and identified themselves as telephone engineers who had come to make adjustments to Mr Haughey's phone. On being admitted, they planted a bugging device in a study room.

The bug remained there for some time, until it was removed following a second garda entry to Mr Haughey's home, again under the Posts and Telegraphs guise. Although Mr Haughey was unaware that his home was being bugged at the time, he subsequently learned of the episode and of the identities of those who carried out the operation.[28]

Three sections of the Garda Síochána have access to electronic surveillance equipment. The first is the Technical Support Section which is located in the Technical Bureau at garda headquarters in the Phoenix Park. This section is involved in obtaining surveillance devices from commercial suppliers in Britain and elsewhere. It also adapts already manufactured equipment to meet the specific operational requirements of under-cover officers in the field which arise from time to time. It was an inspector from the Technical Support Section who oversaw the display to the media in March 1984 of the bugging device found in the Dublin house occasionally used by SDLP politician Seamus Mallon. The assembled reporters were much impressed by the Inspector's thorough knowledge of electronic snooping equipment.

In recent years the Technical Support Section has diversified into video surveillance, including the monitoring by TV cameras of the anti-US President Reagan demonstration in Molesworth Street outside of Dáil Éireann in 1984. Garda video surveillance is now a permanent feature of Cork city, which has six TV cameras around the city centre wired to an elaborate control room at Union Quay barracks.

Although purchased, installed and maintained by Cork Corporation for the purpose of assisting in traffic control, a Cork Corporation official has been quoted as saying that how the video system is used and for what purposes is a matter for the Gardaí. The Cork cameras are alleged to have been deployed on at least two occasions for monitoring political demonstrations: on a march against the Criminal Justice Bill in October 1984 and on protests against the visit to Cork of Israeli President Herzog in June 1985. It is planned to install a similar video surveillance system in Dublin city over the next few years.[29]

The second section with access to bugs is the Intelligence and Security Branch; in particular, C3 division the nerve centre of garda intelligence operations based in the Phoenix Park. It monitors left-wing and anti-establishment groups, foreign diplomats, and domestic subversives. Both bugging and telephone-tapping are used by the ISB maintaining a close familiarity with persons in whom it acquires an interest. The most energetic garda buggers have undoubtedly been the Special Support Unit (SSU) of the Special Task Force (STF). The STF was established in the 1970s as an instant response unit to cope with kidnappings and hi-jackings. Within it, a ten-strong team of detectives came together in an ad-hoc manner to carry out undercover operations of various kinds. This group was later organised on a more formal basis and acquired expertise in electronic surveillance equipment. Although its main targets were the Provisional IRA, this sect-ion has also been involved in monitoring the activities of entirely non-violent organisations, such as the Irish Sovereignty Movement. It is now believed to have been dis-banded.[30]

One bugging operation by the Special Support Section in-volved the surveillance of a flat used by IRA members at Francis Street in Dublin. Conveniently, the shop premises beneath the targeted flat was unoccupied at the time pro-viding the SSU with the opportunity to drill a hole in the floor of the flat and to conceal a bugging device within it. The Provos soon learnt of the covert surveillance and brought down their own 'security' experts from the north, who had perfected their skills against the British army and the SAS.

The Provos identified an office in the nearby Cornmarket area as the base from which the SSU detectives were monitor-ing their flat in Francis Street. Turning the tables, the Provos bugged the SSU observation base. This proved unproductive as most of the SSU conversations picked up referred to code names and code places. They then broke into the private car

of one SSU detective, copied the code books and made the
break-in resemble the work of vandals. The car, a Hillman
Hunter, was parked across the Liffey in Dorset Street at the
time. Having fully flushed out the SSU surveillance, the Provos staged an elaborate decoy operation for several months.
By parading 'interesting' faces in and out of the Francis Street
flat they succeeded in distracting garda attention away from
the arms shipments taking place in other places of the city.

Equally disastrous for the SSU undercover squad was
another bugging operation against the IRA. This time the
scene was Glenageary Road in Dun Laoghaire. The SSU
attempted to bug a flat used by the Provos by drilling a hole
in the separating wall from an adjoining room. As luck would
have it, plaster began to tumble out on top of the assembled
IRA gathering. The alerted Provos chased the SSU men up
Glenageary Road and confiscated the covert surveillance
equipment from the room next door.

Following these two fiascos, the SSU immersed themselves
in the hunt for *Shergar*, the race horse kidnapped allegedly
by the IRA, in 1983. Operation Orange, as is was known, led
an SSU team to County Galway. Again all did not go according
to plan. An amateur radio ham, overhearing the SSU's furtive-
sounding walkie-talkie messages, rang the *Irish Press* in the
mistaken belief that he was picking up Shergar's kidnappers.
The subsequent massive influx of gardaí and media into the
Galway area quickly doomed the Operation Orange undercover exercise.

The activities of the Special Surveillance Unit acquired an
international dimension on at least two occasions, both of
which brought SSU members into direct contact with agents
of MI5, the British Security Services. The first was in 1979,
when a joint Garda-MI5 surveillance operation culminated
in the seizure of an IRA arms' shipment at the Dublin docks.
The weapons had originated in the United States, where a
subsequent court case heard in North Carolina during Sep-

tember of 1980 featured prosecution evidence given by an SSU member and by two MI5 field officers.

The Special Surveillance Unit was also involved in monitoring the movements of staff attached to the Soviet Embassy at Dublin's Orwell Road. When two diplomats and one of their wives were expelled from Ireland for unspecified spying activities in September 1983, it was the SSU in co-operation with Army Intelligence, G2, which led the Irish surveillance effort. Again, the SSU and G2 were both assisted closely in their activities by agents of MI5.

Despite all this frenetic – and not terribly productive – activity, certain detectives are alleged to have managed to find the time and energy to devote to commercial activities of various kinds. How much of this activity was related to undercover work, and how much was purely spare-time entrepreneurship is difficult to establish.

One member operated a company, which has carried out sub-contracted work for a government department. The company was partly financed by bank loans obtained through the mortgaging of two prime apartment properties in Dublin. By coincidence, one of these apartments was allegedly used for a period as an IRA 'safe house', before the Provos realised the identity of their landlord. The detective in question rarely visited these premises in person. The rent was usually collected by a hired agent, whom tenants could only contact through a paging service.

The Moyna Case

It all started when the telephone at the Moyna household went out of order on the morning of Saturday, 29 October 1983.[31] As it was a bank holiday weekend, the fault was not reported until the following Tuesday, at 9.30 a.m. The fault on the telephone line was repaired about an hour later. Aside from the exemplary swiftness of the repair by Telecom Éireann, there was no evidence to suggest that anything out of the ordinary was afoot. Considerations, such as the fact that targeted phone lines are often placed out of order as an excuse to alter line routing at an exchange, simply did not enter anyone's head.

An hour later again, three individuals arrived at the house in a yellow Renault van. Assuming they were here to fix the telephone fault, Mrs Moyna told them, 'It's all right. The phone is fixed.' The eldest-looking of the three replied: 'We've come to fit a new line, we will have to bring the telephone wire in through the back.' Mrs Moyna showed them into the house and they set to work – rewiring.

They started inside the house, laying wires from where the phone was located, through the kitchen and out the window to an ESB pole at the back of the garden. The new wire then travelled across a laneway on to the roof of a stable building and finally down into a drain. Bringing the wire through the kitchen window proved to be something of a problem. One of the men helpfully suggested drilling a hole through the aluminium frame. Mrs Moyna was unimpressed with this idea, so the window had to be left slightly open to accommodate the wire. Their 'rewiring' complete, the three men refused an offer of tea or coffee, saying they had to 'get back to the office'.

When Mr Moyna returned home that Tuesday evening he was dumbfounded by the sight of the work carried out that morning. He resolved to rewire the house in a more professional fashion. Pulling the telephone wire from under the carpet, he discovered it was not connected to the telephone at all; instead, it had a small microphone attached to it. Mr Moyna later pursued the mysterious wire to its other end – an overgrown drain behind the stable building at the rear of the house — and found it linked into a small, square-shaped sealed container. It looked like a miniature radio transmitter.

A relation of Mr Moyna, a graduate in electronic engineering, confirmed that it was.

Mr Moyna consulted his frequent house guest, SDLP politician Seamus Mallon, as to what course of action the family should take. Mr Mallon and Mr Moyna were old friends. They had known each other since footballing days when they had turned out for the Armagh and Monaghan County teams respectively. At the time of the bugging, Seamus Mallon was in Dublin to take part in the deliberations of the New Ireland Forum.

The two agreed that Mr Moyna would draft an account of the whole affair, which Seamus Mallon handed to Taoiseach Garret FitzGerald on 16 November. The statement mentioned that the Moynas had contacted Telecom Éireann and had received an assurance that the three men who had 'rewired' his home were definitely not employees of Telecom.

Two months passed before a garda investigation of the Moyna bugging was completed. The report, which the Taoiseach received on 11 January 1984, showed that the entire garda investigation had limited itself to interviews with the Moyna family and with Telecom Éireann personnel. Dr FitzGerald expressed himself satisfied with the garda investigation. This despite the fact that Mr Moyna and Mr Mallon had made it clear back in November that the bugging had nothing whatsoever to do with Telecom Éireann — and that the culprits were to be found elsewhere.

In February 1984, the *Sunday Tribune* broke the news of the Moyna episode. It described how the bugging operation was carried out and echoed the family's disquiet at the sluggishness and unenergetic nature of the subsequent garda investigation. Now things began to happen – and fast. In the first week of March, Fianna Fáil politician Brian Lenihan named four members of the Special Task Force's Special Support Unit to the Department of Justice and to the media, suggesting that the four 'could be of assistance to any investigation into the bugging affair'. Lenihan claimed he had received this information from an 'anonymous telephone caller'.

Meanwhile two men, both with militant republican backgrounds, were stopped in their car near Heuston railway station by gardaí and questioned about the Moyna bugging. Both later claimed that gardaí had tried to plant bugging equipment on them to implicate the two in the affair. 'I have been framed on the direction of the Minister for Justice,' declared one of the men. The men were placed in an identity parade in front of Mrs Moyna, who remarked afterwards that 'none of the men even remotely resembled the men who had wired the house in November'.

As the case of the Moyna bugging was unfolding, a cousin of the family, Donal Moyna, was arrested along with two others on a charge of possessing explosive substances. The arrest took place in Dundalk on 2 February 1984. The Dundalk arrest could not have come at a more propitious time for the gardaí, if one were to assume that certain officers were desperately trying to cover up any garda involvement in the bugging of the Moyna home. It deflected suspicions entirely in the opposite direction from the gardaí themselves and tainted Mr and Mrs Moyna with involvement in paramilitary activities. Nothing could have been further from the truth.

In the event, the arrest of Donal Moyna proved a disaster for the gardaí. When the case came to trial, independent technical experts described the evidence against him as 'laughable'. All the charges were thrown out. At least Donal Moyna had been given bail while awaiting trial; his two co-accused languished in Portlaoise prison for three months on remand. Neither had any previous convictions. They too had their charges dismissed by the court.

It was during the course of this trial that Mr Moyna's son, Michael Jnr, claimed to have recognised a garda officer as one of the three who had bugged the family home the previous October. The identified man was also one of the four whom Brian Lenihan had named earlier. Michael Moyna Jnr signed an affidavit on his identification on 16 May and submitted it to the secretary of the Department of Justice two weeks later. A subsequent meeting took place concerning the alleged identification of a garda officer involving the Taoiseach, Garret FitzGerald, the secretary of the Department of Foreign Affairs, Seán Donlon, the secretary of the Department of Justice, Andy Ward, the garda commissioner, Laurence Wren and the Minister for Justice, Michael Noonan. Mr Noonan issued a statement saying that the officer concerned was elsewhere at the time and that Michael Moyna Jnr was mistaken in his identification. Mr Michael Moyna Jnr had, with his wife, visited the Killbarrack house during the three hours the 'telephone engineers' were present and had spoken to one of them.

However, for their own reasons the Moyna family decided not to pursue the matter any further with the gardaí and the government.

Two years on, one version of the events behind the Kilbarrack bugging has emerged, if not exactly into public view, then into acceptance among what might be loosely called interested circles. Adherents of this version hold the following view: the Kilbarrack bugging was carried out by individuals who at the time were serving members of the Garda Síochána; it was done at the behest of the British Security Services, MI5; and that the surveillance was directed not at anything relating to New Ireland Forum discussions, rather its purpose was to ascertain whether anything could be found to vilify Mr Mallon.

If MI5 agents were as it is claimed involved, the Kilbarrack episode provides an instructive insight into the grubby world of intelligence operations and underscores the propensity of its protagonists to measure other people's characters by their own. Adherents of this view defend their theories against the charge that whoever planted the bug did so in such a haphazard fashion as to ensure its discovery with the reply that the buggers in question were somewhat less than competent in such activities.

In addition, this school of thought draws comparisons with a second case of bugging, also carried out in Dublin and again targeted at the private life of another visiting senior nationalist politician. Both episodes, it is claimed, were part of an intelligence effort by MI5, carried out on the orders of the British government, to seek potentially embarrassing information about senior politicians, north and south, which might at some future date be used to compromise the individuals concerned.

Certainly, such a plot would not be out of character with previous, documented activities of Her Majesty's secret services. And if it is true, then the most enduring lesson of the Kilbarrack bugging may not be how far certain organisations are willing to go in gathering information; but rather how determined individuals such as Seamus Mallon MP can so inconvenience certain organisations and those behind them, that the mighty British political establishment is driven to pursuing even the most pathetically harebrained of schemes in safe-guarding its interests on this island.

Part III: A Spy in The Sky

Introduction

Official state openings are invariably high spirited affairs, and the formal unveiling in May 1984 of Telecom Éireann's £8 million earth satellite station at Elfordstown, near Midleton in County Cork, was certainly no exception. The symbolic task of cutting the opening ribbon was performed with due ceremony by the attending Minister of State at the Department of Communications, in front of an invited throng of semi-state, departmental, local authority and private industry guests. Well-stocked marquees were provided on-site for the day, wherein hired glasses were raised in a toast to the new project's good health and long life.

The object of all this subsidised jollity beneath the May sunshine was Ireland's first space-age telecommunications station. At its centre stands a huge dish-shaped aerial, pointing skywards from the green fields of east Cork up to an Intelsat V communications satelite, perched 22,300 miles over the Atlantic. By relaying signals off the Intelsat V satellite, Elfordstown can pass telephone calls to and from Ireland with similar ground stations in North America, Africa and the Middle East.

The bringing into operation by Telecom Éireann of the earth station at Elfordstown was not only a technological step forward in its own terms, for the first time ever Ireland was plugged directly into the global telecommunications network. Previously, every single international telephone call, telegram and telex message to or from Ireland had to pass through Britain.[32] As we shall see, this passage of information directly under the electronic noses of British Intelligence

agencies had long proved to be a temptation beyond resist-
ance.

To return to Elfordstown's official opening, one American
individual on the guest list contributed an unusual element
to the day's proceedings by his presence among the marquees.

This individual was Robert Kane, United States Ambassador to Ireland. As Kane socialised with other guests at
Elfordstown, a more publicity-shy team of his fellow country-
men were operating a satellite station of their own, just three
hundred miles away in Cornwall, England. The Cornwall station resembles that at Elfordstown in every respect, just as it
does the other legal, registered Intelsat ground stations dotted
around the rest of the world. However, the Cornwall installation and its sister secret bases are in a somewhat different
line of business: what the Intelsat stations send up to communications satellites, the latter pull back down again.[33] It
could be called space-age phone-tapping; insiders call it Signals Intelligence or SIGINT for short. Its chief practitioners
are the American National Security Agency (NSA), who operate a global network of electronic espionage facilities like
that in Cornwall. To say that the NSA listen to everything
must be an exaggeration, but it would not be a great one.

In the world of international spying and espionage, the
traditional human intelligence gatherers have been pushed
to the sidelines by Signals Intelligence, or SIGINT as it is
known in the jargon. At least 80% of intelligence now
obtained by the major Western powers comes not from the
George Smiley type figures of spy fiction writers like John Le
Carré, but from the global network of electronic eavesdropping stations, relay sites, spy satellites and computers run by
the United States in co-operation with its intelligence
partners. In the words of one commentator – 'Exit Smiley,
enter IBM'.[34]

This part of the book attempts to look inside that secret
world – and analyses how the telecommunications system

of this country is tapped by the SIGINT eavesdroppers.

The SIGINT Wars

If one moment in history could be identified as the time when Signals Intelligence was born, it would be 5 August 1914, the first day of a world war which changed the political map of the globe.[35] A few short hours after England's midnight declaration of war on the German Empire, an equipment-laden ship moved purposively through the North Sea mist. On reaching a point off Emdem, where the German and Dutch coasts meet, the ship dropped grappling hooks overboard and fished intently about in the dark waters for its quarry. The ship was the *Telconia*, a British cable-laying vessel, and it was fishing for Germany's five transatlantic undersea cables, which ran down the English Channel from Emdem. Each of the cables was dragged up, cut and thrown back into the sea; the crew of the *Telconia* repeated the manoeuvre several times, until it was certain that Germany's links with the outside world were severed beyond repair.

It was Britain's first offensive act of the war and not even the Royal Navy who directed the operation fully realised its decisiveness at the time. From that moment on and for the duration of the war, Imperial Germany was sealed off from direct cable contact with the world outside: from its embassies, its consulates and colonies. While cable links still existed with neutral countries such as Sweden and allied ones like Turkey, the Germans were compelled to use radio transmissions for communicating with everywhere else. Radio was a recent innovation at the time, little used except by naval and merchant ships. But by the end of 1914, Germany was flooding the airways with diplomatic and military messages from its huge transmitters at Naeun near Berlin.

And the British were listening to every word. A dozen or

so radio intercept stations were set up around Britain, operated by the Post Office and the Marconi company. All monitored German transmissions were dispatched to Room 40 at
the Admiralty Building in London, where Royal Navy code-
breakers worked around the clock deciphering the intercepts.
In this task, the Room 40 team relied upon three things –
captured German code-books, information from spies and
sheer intellectual genius. As the U-boat war developed and
spread out into the Atlantic, Room 40 established a network
of coastal direction-finding stations, designed to locate the
point of origin of transmissions from German U-boats and
surface ships – and therefore the locations of such vessels.
Five of these stations were set up along the Munster coastline,
under the control of the Vice Admiral, Queenstown (Cobh).
It is estimated that during the course of the war, Room 40
intercepted and decoded some fifteen thousand German
secret communications.

The most celebrated tap of the First World War – perhaps
the greatest SIGINT success of all time – was the capturing
of the so-called Zimmerman Telegram. In January 1917, German Foreign Minister Arthur Zimmerman dispatched a message to his ambassador in Washington, Count Bernstorff. The
message indicated Germany's intention to embark upon total
submarine warfare in the Atlantic, including attacks on
American ships bringing supplies to Britain. The United
States was still neutral at the time, and Zimmerman suggested
that if Germany's action provoked the United States then Germany would seek an anti-United States alliance with Mexico.
Within days of its dispatch, Room 40 had successfully
decoded its own copy of Zimmerman's note. Britain had anxi-
ously sought some means of bringing the United States into
the war: now it had it. The Americans were shown the fateful
message, convinced of its authenticity and compelled to
relinquish their neutral stance. On 6 April, the United States
declared war upon the German Empire.

No other act of Signals Intelligence had such enormous consequences. Had Room 40 not intercepted the Zimmerman note, it is probable that the Germans would have done something else which would have brought America into the war; however, it is also probable that America's entry might have come too late for the allies in Europe. Interestingly, a central part in the Zimmerman affair was played by a cable station on Valentia Island off County Kerry. Reluctant to transmit messages to their Washington Embassy over the airways for fear of interception, the Germans persuaded the Swedish government in 1915 to give them access to a transatlantic cable which ran from Stockholm to Buenos Aires. From here German diplomatic messages were passed to Washington, Mexico and elsewhere – even China. Room 40 quickly learnt of the arrangement and had a tap placed on the Swedish cable as it traversed the west coast of Ireland en route to its junction point on the Canary Islands. A listening post was set up at the cable station on Valentia, operated by Royal Navy telegraphists. Never before or since had so much turned upon a SIGINT tap. For those few moments in time, the eavesdroppers on Valentia Island and the code-breakers of Room 40 held history in the palm of their hand.

Room 40 also intercepted at least thirty-two messages exchanged between Ambassador Bernstorff and his government dealing with German assistance for Sinn Féin. It is not clear how many of these had been decoded before the Easter Rising of 1916, but they provided enough information for Room 40 to follow the main developments of the plot and to set counter-measures in motion. Although the British authorities in Dublin appeared to have been taken by surprise, the Royal Navy was fully prepared: additional ships were despatched to Ireland and marines were landed to protect naval installations and coast guard stations. The marines were also directed to assist the RIC, which they did with great effect. Among those snared in Room 40's trap was Sir Roger

Casement. Taps on the Swedish cable provided them with prior knowledge of Casement's arrival on a German U-boat; when the knighted former servant of the crown turned Irish revolutionary landed on a strand near Tralee, the British were waiting for him.

American Military Intelligence ran its own SIGINT agency during the war. Based in Washington, MI8, as it was known, operated under Herbert Yardley, a bright if eccentric figure who directed the same intellectual brilliance into code-breaking as he had previously invested into mathematics and poker-playing. MI8 also inspected suspicious mails and developed a chemical reagent which brought out secret writing in any form of ink. Among those trapped through this discovery was a colourful German spy who plotted to import high explosives for sabotage inside hollowed statues of saints and the Virgin Mary. After the war, MI8 became know somewhat exotically as the Black Chambers, and its reading of Japanese diplomatic messages during the 1922 Five Nation talks on the tonnage of military vessels was crucial in determining their negotiating position and in producing a Pacific naval balance favourable to the United States.

Between 1917 and 1929, Yardley's SIGINT operators successfully intercepted and read some forty-five thousand secret communications of over a dozen countries, including those of China, the Soviet Union, Brazil, Peru, France, England and Spain. Preliminary analysis had been made of many other codes, among them those of the Vatican. But the end was in sight. President Hoover learned with disapproval of the Black Chambers' activities and had it closed down. In the words of his Secretary-of-State, Henry Stetsom: 'Gentlemen do not read each other's mail.' It was an honourable policy – but a short-lived one. Military necessity would soon see America's code-breakers back at work.

No such gentlemanly niceties interrupted Britain's SIGINT

activities after the First World War. The functions of Room 40 were removed from the Admiralty and transferred to the Secret Intelligence Services, MI6, at their offices in Broadway in the centre of London. Re-named the Government Code and Cipher School (GC&CS), the Signals Intelligence operation kept a particularly close watch on the diplomatic communications of the Soviet Union. In 1927, Prime Minister Baldwin read out intercepted Soviet telegrams in the House of Commons, as proof of his government's claim that the Russians were interfering in British politics and engaging in acts of espionage. As the clouds of war began to darken the skies over Europe in August 1939, the GC&CS moved out of London to Bletchley Park, an ornate mansion fifty miles to the northwest. Conveniently, Bletchley Park was situated half-way between the university towns of Oxford and Cambridge, from where the collective intellectual ability of mathematicians, linguists, classical scholars, radio scientists and chessmasters would soon be summoned to its duty in defence of the realm.

The Allied nations secured victory in the Second World War by virtue of superior military prowess and moral force – or at least so the conventional story goes. In reality, they cheated on a grand and decisive scale. For throughout most of the war, the top-level military radio communications of the Germans, Italians and Japanese were covertly intercepted and decoded by their opponents. The operational strategies of the Axis high commands, what they were saying to each other and to their troops in the field – at crucial stages during the war all were open secrets to the Allies' eavesdropping intelligence agencies. In the words of one SIGINT historian: 'The 1939-1945 war was the first in which one side was regularly privy to the thoughts of the other and could shape its own actions in the light of that knowledge as far as its resources permitted.'[36]

Of all the Allies SIGINT operations, Britain's was beyond

doubt the most sophisticated and successful. By D-Day, some six thousand people were working at Bletchley Park in Buckinghamshire, decoding and analysing the constant stream of Axis military radio signals which poured in from intercept stations dotted around Britain and liberated parts of Europe.

Bletchley was the nerve centre of Britain's SIGINT efforts, and it was here in 1943 that the world's first digital computer was developed to assist in processing the huge volume of intercepted information. It is said that Churchill directed the North African campaign against General Rommel almost exclusively on the basis of information gathered through SIGINT. It is certain that the British Prime Minister, along with President Truman and the senior Allied commanders, would have agreed with General Eisenhower when he remarked in 1945 that in gaining victory for the Allies 'SIGINT was decisive'.

The radio interception and code-breaking triumphs of 1939-1945 were swept up in the great tide of Cold War secrecy. It was not until 1974, when Group Captain F. W. Winterbotham of Bletchley Park obtained after a protracted battle with the authorities permission to publish his wartime memoirs, that the whistle was blown on what was undoubtedly the best kept military secret of this century.[37]

The Global Eavesdroppers

After the war, the British and American intelligence chiefs who were privy to the SIGINT operation against the Axis powers, pushed successfully for a similar joint operation against the new enemy on the other side of the Iron Curtain. A secret Anglo-American agreement was signed in 1947; known as UKUSA pact, it provided for full co-operation on the interception and decoding of foreign radio signals, and for a measure of sharing out of the intelligence results. Canada

and Australia, whose territories were vital in ensuring global
radio interception coverage, were invited to join in the agreement shortly afterwards and did so.

The four nation SIGINT pact is strictly hierarchical in
nature. At the top sits the American National Security Agency
(NSA), whose headquarters are at Fort George Meade, in
Maryland.[38] Under the terms of the 1947 intelligence agreement, all communications intercepted by the three other participating nations must be passed on to the NSA. The Americans, however, are not obliged to make any of their own intelligence available in return and do so purely as they judge
appropriate in the light of their own perceived national
interest.

Britain, through its Cheltenham-based Government Communications Headquarters (GCHQ), has the status of a senior
partner in the transnational SIGINT pact.[39] Second status
partners are Canada's Communications Branch of the
National Research Council (CBNRC), and Australia's Defence
Signals Division (DSD). As part of the 1947 agreement, each
agency has liaison officers inside the headquarters of the
other participants. Some NATO allies, notably Norway and
Germany, are granted third party status. Links have also
existed with Brazil, Sweden and South Africa, among others.
For all its international flavour, Signals Intelligence is very
much an American affair: financed by American dollars,
propelled by American technical innovation and dedicated
pre-eminently to the continued futherance of American military, political and economic interests.

Established by President Harry Truman to co-ordinate and
consolidate the individual electronic espionage efforts of the
army, air force and navy, America's National Security Agency
is truely a remarkable organisation. It commands the largest
single share of that country's intelligence budget and gener-
ates in return a staggering forty tons of classified documents
per day. Employing over one hundred thousand people, the

agency occupies more floor space at its Fort George Meade headquarters alone than any other American government agency except the Pentagon. Fort Meade's eleven acre computer complex is unrivalled in its technological scale and sophistication. Some computers are programmed to break down the communication codes of foreign govenments – allies as well as adversaries – while others systematically scan virtually every international telex, telegram and telephone conversation in search of data of interest. The latter do this by watching for key words and can analyse intercepted communications in this fashion at a rate of four million characters a second. In other words, NSA's Fort Meade computers could read and index a daily newspaper in less than the time it would take the average reader to pronounce its title.

Outside the United States, NSA operates about twenty-five electronic espionage installations: among them San Vito die Normanni in Italy, Pyongraek and Osan in Korea, Sebana Seca in Puerto Rico, Sinop in Turkey, Augsburg in West Germany, Edzell, Chicksands, Menwith Hill and Morwenstow in Britain. Invariably, such bases are described offically as involved in 'radio research', 'atmospheric studies', or the like. On occasion, even the governments which hosted NSA stations were unaware of their true role and function – as the electronic eyes and ears of the largest spy network in the world.

Not the least of NSA's achievements has been its ability to conduct its operations outside public view. Although larger in scale and importance than its sister intelligence organisation, the CIA, for most Americans the National Security Agency does not exist – or is confused with the National Security Council. And that, one assumes, is how the NSA would prefer matters to remain. It was only through the post-Watergate American Congress investigations into the the activities of American intelligence agencies in 1975, that a

corner of the veil which shrouded the NSA for more than
two decades was finally lifted. In the words of Congressman
Church: 'The name (of NSA) is unknown to most
Americans. . . (Yet it) is an immense installation. In its task
of collecting intelligence by intercepting foreign communications, the NSA employs thousands of people and operates
with an enormous budget. . . Its expansive computer facilities
comprise some of the most complex and sophisticated
machinery in the world.' NSA's technology could 'at any time
be turned around on the American people', Senator Church
warned, adding that 'the capacity is there to make tyranny
total.'[40]

Just as the NSA dominates American's espionage
apparatus, Britain's GCHQ provides an estimated 80% of its
country's intelligence information. Over six thousand people
work at its Cheltenham headquarters alone and GCHQ's
annual budget is close to six hundred million pounds;[41] a
figure which exceeds that spent every year on Britain's three
other spy agencies: the Defence Intelligence Staff (DIS), who
monitor intelligence activity under the domain of the Ministry of Defence; MI5, who guard against the activities of foreign
intelligence agencies in Britain and who monitor domestic
anti-establishment groups; and MI6, who direct intelligence-
gathering by British spies abroad.

The British Prime Minister is sent 'important GCHQ intercepts. . . daily in oblong yellow boxes', according to the *Daily
Express* journalist and intelligence expert Chapman
Pincher.[42] But even the country's nominal leader is treated
on a 'need to know basis'. Pincher claims it is GCHQ, and
not the Prime Minister, who decide what information is made
available.

A favourite SIGINT tactic, as Richard Hall explains in his
book on GCHQ's Australian partner, *The Secret State*, is to
keep top-ranking politicians happy by feeding them with distracting low-grade information. When SIGINT finds a 'dip-

lomatic titbit with a Minister's name on it,' says Hall, 'these are almost always pushed forward.'

GCHQ run five listening stations in Britain: Brora in north-eastern Scotland, which eavesdrops upon Soviet military communications; Irton Moor near Scarborough, which listens to communications from Soviet vessels in the North Atlantic: Hacklaw in Fife and Cheadle in Staffordshire, which intercept diplomatic and commerical signals: and Culm Head on the Somerset coast, which relays to Cheltenham messages intercepted by overseas GCHQ stations in Canada, West Germany, Australia, Cyprus, Ascension Island and Ceylon.

The electronic spying operations of the four nation Signal Intelligence agencies have not only increased vastly in scale and extent since the years following the Second World War but they have also changed dramatically in character and emphasis. The high-level communication codes of the Soviet Union are now virtually uncrackable as are those of the United States; although low-grade Eastern Bloc military, diplomatic and economic signals continue to receive close surveillance with apparent success.

As a result, the electronic spies have shifted their resources and attention towards weaker targets: smaller western and third world countries, economic and financial intelligence and – predictably – their own dissident nationals. The American Pike Congressional Committee reported in 1976 that 'communications interception in this (economic) area has developed rapidly since 1972, partly in reaction to the Arab oil embargo and the failure to obtain good information on Russian grain production... for purchase with American corporations'.[43] Current targets include Japan and the Middle Eastern oil-producing nations. Australia's Defence Signals Division regularly broke Japanese communication codes during the 1970s, according to Richard Hall in his book *The Secret State*.

Britain's GCHQ has often advertised for Japanese and

Arabic linguists, and the intelligence it gathers in the economic sphere is made available to selected private industry confidants.

According to Duncan Campbell of the *New Statesman* magazine, GCHQ has had little success in recent years with breaking high-level Soviet communication codes. Consequently, 'SIGINT targets include not just supposedly hostile and unaligned states, but also Britain's putative friends and allies.'

The Americans, too, bug their friends. In the 1960s an offical at the French Embassy in Washington was bribed to turn his back while the NSA stole, duplicated and returned the magnetic tapes which held the keys to France's diplomatic codes. A 1975 American government report, declassified in error by the authorities revealed that NSA even taps what the report called America's 'closest ally' – Britain. According to the Fink report to the House Committee on Government Operations and Individual Rights 'NSA monitors the traffic of specific countries, including Great Britain, our closest ally.'[44] Two years previously a former NSA analyst told the American magazine *Ramparts* that: 'The allies can't maintain security even if they want to. They're working with the machines we gave them. Chicksands (an NSA base in England) does everybody in Europe. There is a lot of overlap. Brindisi (at San Vito dei Normanni, Italy) does just about everybody in Europe in overlap also.'

Another feature of NSA's activities which emerged in American Congress investigations during the mid-1970s, was the agency's spying on anti-establishment groups and individuals, at home and abroad. By 1974, the NSA had built up computer dossiers through communications-monitoring on some seventy-five thousand American citizens; including former Attorney-General Robert Kennedy, civil rights leader Martin Luther King, and anti-Vietnam war campaigners such as Jane Fonda and Dr Benjamin Spock.

According to the Church Committee of the American Congress, NSA's watch list included 'prominent Americans in business, the performing arts and politics, including members of Congress'. The Committee went on to note that 'the great majority of names on the (NSA tapping) watch list have always been foreign citizens and organisations', who like their American counter-parts, are 'members of radical political groups, from celebrities to ordinary citizens involved in protest against their government.'

Tapping Ireland

In January 1987, the *Irish Times* reported that Britain's GCHQ regularly intercepts diplomatic radio messages sent to and from Irish embassies. Quoting 'high-level sources', the report claimed that electronic surveillance was particularly intense during the negotiations leading up to the Anglo-Irish Agreement of December 1985. So serious was the situation that all sensitive material concerning the negotiations was either carried to and from London by diplomats, or given to Aer Lingus pilots to bring across the Irish Sea. Improved relations between the Dublin and London governments since the signing of the Agreement has not meant any lessening in GCHQ's surveillance of Irish radio, telex and telephone messages, the report continued.

If, as is claimed, confidential Irish government communications are subjected to habitual surveillance by GCHQ and its SIGINT partner NSA, they certainly possess every opportunity and technical means to do so. Confidential messages to and from this country's sixty foreign embassies are wide open to tapping by the SIGINT agencies, whether they pass by radio transmission or along commercial telephone and telex. And not alone are the international communications of the Irish government routinely bugged by GCHQ and NSA, those of its citizens are just as closely – and as covertly – monitored.

Three ways exist in which any government can hope to communicate securely with its representatives in foreign countries. The first, and most reliably secure from clandestine interference, is what is known as the 'diplomatic bag': a sealed pouch which is dispatched, accompanied by a trusted functionary who carries it often hand-cuffed to his or her wrist, directly by air or sea to its point of destination. Such 'diplomatic bags' are exempted from customs' examination under international law. Although secure they are slow and cumbersome.

A second, and instantaneous method, is by 'diplomatic telegram' – telex messages sent along conventional telecommunications lines, which are encoded by scrambler devices to guard against unauthorised persons or organisations acquainting themselves with their contents. This method is the most widely used by governments, including our own. The strength of diplomatic telegrams' security against tapping depends wholly upon the impenetrability of the codes used to hide their contents. The same is true of radio communications, which is method number three. According to the *Irish Times* report, the codes used in Irish diplomatic communications, generated on a £1 million, Swiss-made scrambler device, have been broken by GCHQ.

A high-power radio antenna was installed on top of the Department of Foreign Affairs Building Iveagh House, in St Stephen's Green in Dublin in the 1970s, and is used regularly to exchange diplomatic messages with Irish embassies abroad. The Department of Defence also operates its own radio service from its Parkgate Street headquarters, through which it communicates with Irish troops on United Nations duty overseas. As might be expected, all these communications are routinely monitored by GCHQ and NSA. After all, radio transmissions are available to be plucked out of the sky by any or all who care to listen in – and there exists no better equipped or keener listeners than the SIGINT agencies.

Four British GCHQ stations were involved in spying on Irish government radio communications; now there are just three. The fourth was Gilnahirk Government Signal Overseas Station in east Belfast – closed since 1978.[45] One of the 250 former employees there told the *Sunday Tribune* in 1982 that the station was used to intercept 'all transmissions from the Irish stations in Iveagh House and Parkgate'. Gilnahirk also tapped Irish diplomatic telegrams which were routed via the North he claimed.

Three GCHQ stations currently monitor Irish government communications.[46] Two of these intercept Department of Foreign Affairs and Defence radio transmissions; the third monitors diplomatic messages sent through the international telephone and telex networks. One of the pair of radio intercept stations is Hacklaw, at Cupar in Fife. This Scottish station has been in operation since the Second World War, when it plucked from the skies signals from Lufftwafte aircraft and relayed them to Bletchley Park. Today, Hacklaw is controlled by the UK Composite Signals Organisation, the civilian agency of GCHQ, and reports to Cheltenham. Hacklaw eavesdrops upon the communications of Warsaw Pact countries, NATO allies, and neutral nations such as Sweden and Ireland.

Working in tandem with Hacklaw is another GCHQ station, this time located in England. Two stations are required to guarantee total coverage, due to a technical affect of long-distance communications known as the 'skip'. The station is at Cheadle in Staffordshire, some fifty miles south of Manchester. It was at Cheadle in 1969 that the most successful spy to work inside GCHQ, Soviet mole Geoffrey Prime, began his thirteen year career of passing SIGINT secrets to his foreign paymasters.

Irish government messages sent through the conventional

telephone and telex system are subjected to an elaborate tapping system, organised from a British Telecom building in the centre of London. Engineers at Caroone House, on Farringdon Street in the City of Westminster, control the interception of all international calls and telexes passing through Britain. All these communications must go through seven international exchanges in central London. The engineers place tape recorders on selected lines at these exchanges and hand over the raw data to GCHQ at Cheltenham for analysis. Technology developed by GCHQ enables all such intercepted traffic to be converted into digital form to facilitate computer searches through large numbers of telephone conversations for items of interest. For example, all calls made to or from specified numbers, all calls in which a specified word is mentioned or where the voice of a specified person is overheard.

Britain's phone-tapping legislation has been specially framed to accommodate this large-scale monitoring of international communications. In the case of domestic telephone taps,the 1984 Interception of Communications Bill requires that warrants may be issued only to cover the specified phone lines of named persons or organisations. However, a clause in the Bill exempts from this requirement warrants issued by the Foreign Secretary for 'external (international) communications' in support of 'its defence and foreign policies'. Effectively, this gives the British government carte blanche to trawl through literally thousands of international telephone conversations and telex messages.

When Ireland's international telecommunications are intercepted travelling by radio or along commercial telephone lines, they all end up at the one location: K Division, GCHQ, Oakley Priors Road, Cheltenham.

This section handles all monitored communications from non-Soviet bloc countries, plus intercepted commercial messages. An estimated fifty to sixty of its staff are dedicated specifically to analysing Irish communications. They are assisted in their work by the code-breakers in H Division, who are in turn supported by X Division. This latter operates one of Britain's largest single computer complexes, reputed to use as much electricity as a medium-sized town.

The intelligence dossiers prepared by K Division's analysts go to two places. Firstly, across to the other side of Cheltenham town to Benhall Park, location of the American National Security Agency's liaison office in Britain, as is required under the 1947 Anglo-American pact on intelligence data-sharing. The other destination is Britain's Joint Intelligence Committee (JIC).[47] Part of the cabinet office, JIC has its own 'ambassadors' to the three other participating nations in the transnational SIGINT agreement, in addition to representatives from GCHQ, MI5, MI6, and the Defence Intelligence Service. Normally, the CIA's station chief in London and his Canadian and Australian counterparts sit in at the weekly JIC meetings. They withdraw, however, for what is coyly described as 'domestic' business. JIC also includes staff from the Departments of Trade, Industry and Energy, who specialise in economic intelligence.

Ironically, the systematic tapping of Irish government communications by GCHQ is liable to have compromised Irish state security to the Soviet Union, the very country GCHQ was established to spy against. For although GCHQ has long been successful in keeping its activities secret from the British public, it has achieved substantially less success in preventing infiltration by Soviet agents or 'moles'. For there have only been seven years in GCHQ's forty-year long history when there has not been a Russian spy working inside it. The most recent and celebrated Soviet agent within GCHQ was Geoffrey Prime, who was apprehended in 1982 having spent thirteen years passing information to the Russians.[48] GCHQ's appalling security record has led NSA officers to describe the agency as of 'more use to Russian than Britain's allies'. So while GCHQ's monitoring of Irish government secrets has been of inestimable value to Britain's intelligence chiefs, paradoxically, the KGB in Moscow's Dzerzhinsky Square may have found it of considerable assistance as well.

In addition to the laying bare of confidential Irish government, diplomatic and military messages, all personal and commercial communications between Ireland and the rest of the world are similarly monitored by the SIGINT tappers.

All of this country's telecommunications with the world at large (with the exception of the Elfordstown satellite station) must first pass through Britain, directly under the electronic noses of GCHQ and NSA's British bases.

Two pairs of submarine telephone cables run out from Dublin's North Bull Island and Howth Harbour to the Welsh coast, and a microwave radio station on top of Three Rock Mountain to the south of the city feeds into a similar station at Holyhead on Anglesey. A proportion of the Republic's international telecommunications also pass via the north. Either along submarine cables from Ballyhornan and Donaghdee in Co. Down; or through microwave stations at St John's Point in Co. Down or at Ballygormartin on the western outskirts of Belfast. Once picked up at their terminals on the other side of the Irish Sea, these links are switched through to their eventual destinations. In the case of in-coming communications from Britain or beyond, the system simply operates in reverse.

As might be expected, telephone conversations between Britain and all parts of Ireland receive particularly close scrutiny. In October 1982 *The Sunday Times* revealed that the NSA Menwith Hill station in Yorkshire taps all communications links crossing the Irish Sea and stores much of the information obtained in its computer banks. According to the report, telephone intercepts that may be of value in combating Irish paramilitary activity on the British mainland are passed on to the UK Security Services (MI5).

Duncan Campbell has reported in the *New Statesman* that Menwith Hill personnel go on full alert immediately after an

IRA bomb attack or other paramilitary activity in Britain. The timing is revealing – and it is not the base guards who go on overtime, but the communication analysts. Their job, an NSA official in Washington told Campbell, is to sift through already recorded telephone conversations between Britain and all parts of Ireland in search of clues concerning a forth-coming attack. 'Tape is cheap,' the official explained, 'storing an hour's calls on a 1,000 line link is simple and would cost less than $100 worth of tape.'

So it would appear that although all phone calls across the Irish Sea are intercepted and stored for a period of time on computer files, it is only on these occasions when they might be judged likely to yield information of security value that they are subjected to full human restrospective analysis; in particular, in the immediate aftermath of paramilitary activity in Britain. Some experts see NSA's involvement in the anti-IRA campaign as an inexpensive gesture made in return for the extraordinary facilities which the American intelligence agency has been provided by the British, and one calculated to make its presence there more palatable to the host government.

Along with this periodic blanket surveillance of communications links across the Irish Sea, it would be surprising indeed if the standard NSA watch-list procedure is not applied to telephone conversations between Ireland and Britain. That is to say, calls between certain phone numbers would be intercepted and analysed on a regular or permanent basis. Similarly, Menwith Hill's voice recognition computer systems would be programmed to scan all Irish-British telecommunications links for phone conversations between targeted individuals.

Obvious candidates for such special attention would of course be suspected paramilitaries and subversives, and other politically troublesome individuals and organisations. But if NSA practice elsewhere is any guide, the Irish-Britain

intercept watch-list would in addition embrace key establishment figures and decision-makers. Interesting information
obtained would in turn be made available to the relevant
British/American intelligence, economic and political
authorities or perhaps stored on site, in what one former
British military officer who visited Menwith Hill described
as 'a computer file dossier on European political and trade
union leaders'.[49]

Communications between Ireland and the international
world beyond Britain are no less vulnerable to clandestine
tapping.

Menwith Hill would also be responsible for intercepting
communications from Britain to Scandinavia, continental
Europe, Africa and beyond. The task of monitoring transatlantic links between Britain and the Americans falls upon
another SIGINT installation — Morwenstow, located on the
cliffs of Sharpnose Point, just north of Bude town in Cornwall.
In the words of a former NSA officer, 'there are three satellites
over the Atlantic, each capable of transmitting on about
20,000 circuits. There are eight transatlantic cables with
about 5,000 circuits. NSA monitors all these circuits, collects
and records the electronic information transmitted, and its
computers can pick out the message it wants by "key
words".'[50]

Morwenstow is a joint British/American base; its twin ninety
seven foot satellite snooping dishes have been nicknamed by
insiders as 'Pat' and 'Louis', in honour of former NSA
directors. Its tapping capacity is believed to include access
to transatlantic submarine cables which come ashore at other
parts of the Cornish coast. Some of these oceanic cables, and
the nearby Goonhilly Downs British Telecom earth satellite
station, were partly financed by the Irish Department of Post
and Telegraphs, in return for their use in carrying Ireland's
international communications.

As with Menwith Hill, there are far too many voice channels for Morwenstow's eavesdroppers to monitor every call; but everything 'written' — telex, telegrams, data and fac- simile — is routinely scanned, according to Duncan Campbell. And with the aid of huge American-built comput- ers, Morwenstow can pick out telephone conversations between targeted numbers and individuals to be listened to continually or at random.

The operation of the Telecom Éireann satellite station at Elfordstown, and its independent direct link to the Intelsat system is unlikely to be a cause of any great inconvenience to the tappers. Morwenstow intercepts signals as they 'bounce' off the sky-borne satellites, and not as they leave, or are received by, ground stations. In other words, whatever Telecom Éireann send up from Elfordstown 'Pat' and 'Louis' can pull back down again for computer or human analysis, or both.[51]

Does the Soviet Union also operate a Signals Intelligence system and are Irish telecommunications spied upon by the Soviets? Certainly, the Soviet Union operates a considerable Signals Intelligence network; however, geographical con- straints severely hamper its capabilities to spy upon countries like Ireland which are distant from its borders. With the exception of listening posts in a few client states such as Cuba, Angola and Vietnam, the Soviets have never obtained the global facilities necessary to carry out the type of blanket radio interception so long practised by the United States and its SIGINT allies. Similarly, they do not have the land-based tracking and communications stations needed to remain in constant touch with satellite 'spies-in-the-sky'.

While much long-distance diplomatic and military com- munications transmitted on high-frequency radio bands can be intercepted from inside the USSR and the Eastern Bloc, the Soviets have had to develop a two-prong strategy to monitor the short-range VHF signals and internal telephone calls of other nations. Method number one is to place listening

posts inside their embassies abroad. Their second method is
to construct special ships containing electronic surveillance
equipment and station them off the coasts of countries in
which they develop an interest.

These electronic espionage ships are known in NATO par-
lance as AGIs — Auxiliary General Intelligence vessels. The
nearest one to our shores is what the Royal Navy has nicknamed as the 'Malin Head AGI'. This is not a single vessel,
but a reference to whichever of the Soviet Navy's fifteen
Okean-class surveillance ships is moored off the north
Donegal coast at a particular time; there has been a permanent
presence there since the late 1970s.[52] The Malin Head AGI
monitors the passage of American submarines in and out of
their Scottish forward base at Holy Loch. It also eavesdrops
on the radio communications of the British army and RUC
in the six counties. In addition, British Ministry of Defence
sources have been quoted as saying that Soviet submarines,
which patrol regularly in the Irish Sea, monitor a radio communications link running from the NATO Early Warning
Radar Station at Bishopscourt in County Down to military
command centres in England and Belgium.

Any suitably equipped Soviet vessel stationed off the
coasts of the Republic should also be able to monitor a wide
variety of communications traffic. Among the likely targets
of interest would be messages transmitted on garda and army
radio networks, and car-phones used by other diplomats here.
A Soviet AGI would in addition have access to the literally
thousands of Irish trunk telephone conversations which are
carried every day on Telecom Éireann's microwave radio system. For example, any of the huge number of circuits carried
by the transmitter at Dame Court in the centre of Dublin could
readily be picked up, as could telephone calls sent across the
Irish Sea via transmitters at Three Rock Mountain in south
County Dublin and Holyhead in Wales.

The Soviet's ability to intercept the domestic phone calls

of other countries was clearly demonstrated in the case of
British double agent, Peter Edge. In the early 1980s, Edge was
paid by the British Security Services, MI5, to visit East Germany and to pass on false information to the authorities there,
who believed him to be working for them. Edge's operations
were abruptly cancelled in 1983, after he had made a phone
call discussing his work from Bristol to London. MI5 told
Edge his call went not by underground cable but by microwave radio and that the Soviets routinely intercept such calls.
Edge was warned not to go back to East Germany as his life
would be in danger.[53]

A less exotic – and less expensive – way of monitoring
other nations' telephone calls is to operate SIGINT stations
from inside embassies. Without doubt, the most celebrated
instance of the Soviets exploiting an overseas embassy for
SIGINT purposes was the so-called Microwave Alley
affair. The Soviet embassy in question houses their ambassador to the United Nations and is located on a thirty-seven
acre site in the Glencove suburb of Long Island, New York.
The embassy faces out on Long Island Sound, a stretch of
water across which is beamed on microwave radio some of
America's most sensitive telephone communications links;
hence its nickname, Microwave Alley. By using electronic
eavesdropping equipment, the Soviets were – and still are –
able to monitor the communications of various American
government departments, including the Department of
Defence, major military contractors, plus virtually every long-
distance telephone conversation originating in the north-
eastern states.

The whistle was blown on the SIGINT taps at Glencove by
the highest-ranking Soviet official ever to defect to the west,
their former United Nations Under Secretary, Arkady Schev-
chenko. He revealed that 'at least fifteen to seventeen technicians (were) working on the job' and that 'several tons' of
intercepted material were shipped back to Moscow annually

for analysis. According to a one time CIA officer, the Soviets
were able to pull off their famous 1972 grain coup – in which
they obtained some twenty million tons of American grain
at subsidised prices – by tapping the Department of Agricul-
ture telephones. 'They ended up knowing more about the
American grain market than we did,' he said. For their part,
the Soviets continue to deny everything. Short of encoding
even the lowliest of government telephone calls, there is little
if anything the American government – or any government
– can do to combat such abuse of diplomatic privilege. It was
left to the local Long Island Community Council to take
matters into their own hands; the area's forty-five thousand
residents voted in 1982 to ban the devious Soviets from using
local beaches, tennis courts and golf courses.[54]

The vast bulk of SIGINT eavesdropping operations are
illegal. The interception of government diplomatic communications, of whatever kind, is contrary to international law; in
particular, it breaches the Vienna Convention on Diplomatic
Relations. While the Geneva International Telecommunications Convention binds every country to safeguard the
privacy of all international electronic communications such
obligations are, however, as unenforceable as they are high-
minded, and not taken too seriously by the SIGINT powers.
According to one report, the Chicksands NSA base in Britain
has a copy of the Geneva International Telecommunications
Convention pasted upside down on one of its walls — a sort
of tappers in-joke.

No small nation such as Ireland can hope to escape the
attention of the SIGINT eavesdroppers. Any form of confidential government communications, whether sent by radio, telephone or telex, is liable to be read like an open book.
In terms of international negotiations with foreign powers –
EEC members, the United States or whoever – the old phrase
of 'going naked into the conference chamber' is one that readily comes to mind. For how can one hope to negotiate success-

fully with the other side when they know one's bottom line? The best that can be done in such circumstances is to keep as close an eye on the others as they do on you. Encouragingly, much good work continues to be done in this area; it is one form of state surveillance at which the citizen cannot baulk.

Notes

1. *Sunday Independent,* 16 January 1972
2. *Magill,* December 1980
3. I am indebted to an account of the history of telephone-tapping in Ireland to two lengthy articles by Joe MacAnthony which appeared in the *Sunday Independent,* 9 and 16 January 1972
4. T. Ryle Dwyer, *Sunday Independent,* 17 June 1984
5. MI5, Nigel West, Granada, London 1983
6. For details of those phones which were tapped in the 1973-1980 period, see *Magill,* December 1980
7. *Sunday World,* 23 January 1983
8. The use of phone-taps in the Somerville and Tidey kidnappings is described in *Phoenix,* 19 August 1983 and 20 January 1984
9. For a description of the role of the Investigation Section in phone-tapping, see the *Irish Times,* 1 February 1980, *Hibernia,* 7 February 1980 and *New Hibernia,* November 1985
10. *Operation Brogue,* John M. Feehan, The Mercier Press, Cork and Dublin 1984
11. *Magill,* December 1980
12. For an exhaustive account of phone-tapping technology, see *Magill* December 1980; see also *Tapping the Telephone,* Post Office Engineering Workers Union, London 1980 and *Technocop,* British Society for Social Responsibility in Science, Free Association Books, London, 1985
13. The history of legislation surrounding phone-tapping is described in *Tapping the Telephone;* see also *In Dublin,* January 1983
14. See the *Sunday World,* 11 June 1978 and *Hibernia,* 15 June 1978
15. *New Hibernia,* December 1985 and January 1986; see also *Business and Finance,* May 1986
16. *Ibid.*
17. *Ibid.*
18. *Irish Press,* 20 November 1981 and *Phoenix,* 19 August 1983
19. *Sunday Tribune,* 15 March 1981
20. *Success,* February 1983
21. *Sunday Tribune,* 15 March 1981
22. *Phoenix,* 25 May 1984
23. For a detailed analysis of bugging technology, see *Spy Tech,* Graham Yost, Harrap, London 1985 and *The Complete Spy: An Insider's Guide To The Latest In High Tech Espionage and Equipment,* Robert McGarney and Elise Caitlin, Perigle Books, New York,

1983. Authorative articles on the subject are to be found in *Wireless World*, December 1973, *Electronics Today International*, January 1978, *New Scientist*, 23 November 1978 and *Science Now*, March 1983

24. *Phoenix*, 18 February 1983
25. *Sunday Tribune*, 1 February 1981
26. *Success*, February 1983
27. *Sunday Tribune*, 26 February 1984
28. *Ibid*
29. *Hot Press*, 5 May 1986
30. The activities of the garda SSU are chronicled in *Phoenix*, 1 April 1983, 2 March 1984, 16 March 1984, 7 June 1984, 20 July 1984 and 26 October 1984; see also the *Sunday Independent*, 18 September 1983
31. For a thorough analysis of the Moyna bugging, the subsequent garda investigation and the prosecution of Donal Moyna, see the *Sunday Tribune*, 26 February 1984 and 3 June 1984. The details of the arrest of Donal Moyna are given in *Phoenix*, 11 May 1984 and 22 June 1984. Michael Moyna Junior's claim about one of the Kilbarrack tappers is reported in the *Sunday Tribune*, 3 June 1984 and in the *Irish Times*, 4 June 1984
32. Elfordstown's role in Ireland's international telecommunications is described in *Technology Ireland*, June 1984
33. *Sunday Times*, 14 March 1981
34. *Sunday Times*, 31 October 1982
35. For a comprehensive history of SIGINT activities during the First World War, see *The Code Breakers*, David Kahn, Weidenfeld & Nicholson, London 1966; see also *The Zimmerman Telegraph*, Barbara Tuchman, Constable, London 1959, and *Room 40: British Naval Intelligence 1914-1918*, Patrick Beesly, Oxford University Press, 1982
36. *ULTRA in the West*, Ralph Bennett, Hutchinson, London, 1979
37. For further accounts of Bletchley Park during the Second World War, see *The Hut Six Story*, Gordon Welchman, Penguin, London 1982, and *Top Secret ULTRA*, Peter Calvocoressi, Cassel, London 1980
38. For an in-depth study of the American National Security Agency, see *The Puzzle Palace*, James Bamford, Sidgwick & Jackson, London, 1983
39. The close relationship between America's NSA and Britain's GCHQ is explored in *The Unsinkable Aircraft Carrier*, Duncan Campbell, Michael Joseph, London 1984.
40. *New Statesman*, 2 February 1979 and 18 July 1980
41. For details of GCHQ's scale and funding see *The Observer*, 3 February 1985
42. *New Statesman*, 2 February 1979

43. The Pike Report is published by Spokesman Books, Nottingham, 1977
44. The Fink Report is cited in the *New Statesman*, 25 July 1980
45. The Gilnakirk tapping station is described in the *Sunday Tribune*, 18 July 1982
46. For a detailed study of GCHQ stations and their eavesdropping targets, see the *New Scientist*, 5 April 1984. GCHQ's London facilities are further described in the *New Scientist*, 28 February, 1985
47. Britain's Joint Intelligence Committee is analysed in the *New Statesman*, 19 November 1982
48. For details of Geoffrey Prime's career inside GCHQ, see *The Guardian*, 11 November 1982
49. For details of Menwith Hill NSA base and its tapping of Irish telephone calls see the *New Statesman*, 18 July 1980 and the *Sunday Times*, 31 October 1982
50. *New Statesman*, 18 July 1980
51. See *The Unsinkable Aircraft Carrier*, Duncan Cambell, Michael Joseph, London, 1984
52. For a description of Soviet AGI activities off the Irish coast, see *War Machine*, magazine, No.100, Orbis Publishing, London 1985, and *Anti-Submarine Warfare*, Rear Admiral J. R. Hill, Ian Allen, London 1984
53. *The Observer*, 7 October 1984
54. *The Guardian*, 6 September 1982

THE SECRET WAR

An Account of the Sinister Activities along the Border involving Gardai, RUC, British Army and the SAS
Patsy McArdle

— Why have most politicians chosen to ignore fundamental human rights violations in border areas?

— Are the Dublin governments operating a double moral standard — on the one hand condemning torture in the north and on the other allowing horrific things to happen within the walls of garda stations?

— Are the Irish army supporting the paratroopers and SAS?

— Why are heavily armed SAS men, if arrested, not treated as terrorists in the Dublin courts?

— How have photographs taken by the gardai during interrogation of alleged suspects ended up in the hands of the security forces in the north?

— Is information being given to the RUC being passed on to the UVF?

— Why is the co-operation so one-sided?

— Is the IRA the cause of the violence or are they only responding to British aggression and loyalist repression of the minority in the north?

— Are the people living along the border disillusioned by political rethoric?

OPERATION BROGUE
John M. Feehan

— *Operation Brogue* examines some recent events in the political life of Charles J. Haughey and questions the role played by the British Secret Service in the campaign of denigration against him believed to have been given the code-name *Operation Brogue*.

— It looks at the reasons why the British would want to destroy Mr Haughey in the context of their military needs to extend their strategic influence throughout the Republic.

— It explores the danger posed to these British strategic interests by Mr Haughey and his unwillingness to allow the Republic to be exploited by outside interests or to be made subservient to them.

— It outlines a number of standard techniques used by the British to mould people of standing and influence to their way of thinking

— It considers how far the media gave a one-sided account of events to the detriment of Mr Haughey and suggests a lot of pertinent questions which they should have asked but did not.

— Finally it looks at Mr Haughey's role in the future and examines the question as to whether he is the person to lead the country out of its present state of near despair.

THE STALKER AFFAIR
Frank Doherty

* Would the whole system of covert cross-border co-operation be threatened if what went on in the Republic in the run up to the deaths of Grew and Carroll became known?

* Was Stalker about to uncover one of British intelligence's most closely guarded secrets — the penetration of the garda siochana?

* Would the exposure of the Badger (a British agent in the gardai) reveal MI5's involvement in illegal covert operations directed not only against the IRA but also leading Irish politicians?

* Is there official Irish connivance with British covert operations in the South?

* How close did Stalker come to implicating Margaret Thatcher in his enquiry?

THE STATESMAN
John M. Feehan

This book is in the nature of a sequel to the author's best-selling *Operation Brogue*. It poses many startling questions:

* Is Haughey the statesman who can pull Ireland out of its mood of despair?

* Can he revive the national spirit and destory the British grip on our political life?

* Can he break the power of the British Secret Service in the Republic?

* Are the Coalition bringing us close to Civil War?

* What steps are MI6 likely to take to vilify and break him?

These and many other questions are dealt with in this penetrating and fascinating new book which is sure to become as good a bestseller as *Operation Brogue*.

THE RISE AND DECLINE OF FIANNA FAIL
Kevin Boland

Fianna Fail was once a proud, idealistic and disciplined party whose first aim was 'to secure the unity and independence of Ireland as a Republic.'

— Has this aim become merely a catch-cry or has it become so important as an aim in itself that it is seen as a necessary permanent feature of Fianna Fail policy — because the accomplishment of the aim, if achieved, would make the sub-title 'The Republican Party' obsolete?

— Having secured 'the removal of the government subservient to the foreign master', have Fianna Fail now decided that they are 'under contract with the enemy to maintain his overlordship' in Northern Ireland?

— Have Fianna Fail rejected the idea that Partition is perhaps the gravest injury one nation can inflict on another?

— Has the loss of Fianna Fail's Republican principles been replaced by selfish materialism?

— Has Fianna Fail's revered principle of unconditional loyalty to an individual rather than to a national policy made it a party of people conditioned to act only as automatons and not to think for themselves?

— Has there been a complete reversal of the policies on which Fianna Fail was founded — and if so is disintegration the only future ahead for the party?

FINE GAEL: BRITISH OR IRISH?
Kevin Boland

— Is the excessive zeal in the repression of its enemies one of the main factors inhibiting real public confidence in Fine Gael of the order required for an overall majority?

— Is the complete ruthlessness in the suppression of Republicans still a fundamental part   of the party's policy?

— Is the present day party dedicated to getting the people to proclaim in their Constitution that the claim to national unity is not based on the principles of democracy and justice but is a mere aspiration rightfully subjected to the armed veto of a dissident minority — even when we are told that force acheives nothing?

— Do Fine Gael consider themselves enlightened realists against thick-headed diehards, the upholders of law and order against rebels and subversives, of peace against violence?